KNITTED SCARVES

press

Pam Powers

STACKPOLE
BOOKS

0 11557 01328 3

Published by
STACKPOLE BOOKS
5067 Ritter Road
Mechanicsburg, PA 17055
www.stackpolebooks.com

Printed in United States of America

10 9 8 7 6 5 4 3 2 1

First edition

Cover design by Caroline Stover
Project and model photography by Misty Matz
How-to photography by Kevin Kato and Claire Powers

Library of Congress Cataloging-in-Publication Data

Powers, Pam.
  Dress-to-impress knitted scarves : 24 extraordinary designs for kerchiefs, cowls, infinity loops, & more / Pam Powers. — First edition.
     pages cm
  ISBN 978-0-8117-1328-3
1. Knitting—Patterns. 2. Scarves. I. Title.
  TT825.P6888 2015
  746.43'2—dc23
                                        2014028763

Contents

Introduction

Like many women of my generation, I learned to knit as a child, taught by my grand-mother who, despite her chronic arthritis, knit sweaters, ponchos, and accessories for me. I took a long hiatus through my adolescence and adulthood, but came back to knitting after visiting my local yarn store and picking up an issue of *Rowan* magazine. I was amazed at the beautiful, fashionable designs and presentation. It wasn't long before I began adapting knitting patterns to suit my taste, then designing my own garments and accessories.

For most knitters, the scarf is their first knitting project. A scarf can be simple and small, and the time investment yields the perfect, wearable accessory. I, personally, LOVE scarves! You can really showcase lovely stitch patterns and clever construction without having to worry too much about size and fit. I believe that if you are taking the time and expense to hand knit an accessory, it should be special in some way and not just a scarf that you could buy at the mall for probably less than what you would pay for the yarn. Scarves can really be statement pieces with an outfit. I'll show you pieces that work perfectly with dresses and more formal outfits, but could also be transitioned into winter wear with a sweater and coat. These distinctive scarves also make unique and thoughtful handmade gifts.

In this book I have put together a collection of scarves, cowls, infinity loops, and ascots all with unique design elements. So often the conception of a design will start with a theme, whether it be inspired by a technique, stitch pattern, fiber, or shape, and several interpretations will grow from that initial idea. So rather than having to narrow down each concept to one scarf, I am presenting the pieces in pairs that showcase their creative commonality.

When I construct accessories, I start with an idea of how it will be worn with a certain type of outfit. I then map out a shape, stitch pattern, and any other decorative elements like edgings or buttonholes. I believe that extra finishing touches like diagonal ends or scalloped button loops set these scarves apart from garments you would buy in the store, and it is worth the time to learn these techniques. I've shown the pieces on the models worn wrapped, looped, buttoned, and clasped the way I envisioned them when I first sketched out the design, but feel free to play with the garments and come up with new configurations. I've also included photos for several of the pieces showing different ways you can wear them.

Please take the time to read through the pattern completely before beginning a project. I have included a section, How to Read My Patterns (page 128), that will be helpful in getting started. You are on your way to making lovely, one-of-a-kind accessories!

Happy knitting!

Ruffles & Ruching

The first pattern I ever published was the Ruffled & Ruched Scarf. I have literally sold thousands of copies of this pattern, and have not yet gone to a trade show or knitting event where I did not see either someone wearing this scarf or the scarf on display in a yarn company booth. These two patterns are hybrids of that original design. Both pieces have a sweet style that works with dresses and feminine-style coats.

Shirring Cowl

The Shirring Cowl, at first glance, looks almost identical to Ruffled & Ruched, but actually differs significantly in size and technique. It is longer and more "ruffled" and "ruched," the result of a lot more increases and decreases. Shirring Cowl is worked from the outer two edges inward, as opposed to Ruffled & Ruched, which is worked from the center out. The two halves are then joined together in the center using a 3-needle bind-off, which secures the ruching and keeps it from stretching out over time.

Gossamer Layered Scarf

Gossamer Layered Scarf consists of a base rectangle, knit up in seed stitch using soft baby alpaca, which is layered with ruffled and ruched sections worked in an ethereal mohair yarn. The two layers are joined in two places using a 3-needle join, and finally the center is joined with a 3-needle bind-off. The two ties are worked with stitches picked up along both edges of the center and are finished with short-row–formed beveled ends.

Shirring
Cowl

FINISHED MEASUREMENTS
8"/20.5 cm wide and 31"/79 cm long

YARN
330 yds/302 m worsted weight #4 yarn (shown in
#1946 Silver, Cascade 128 Superwash; 100% super-
wash merino wool; 128 yds/117 m per 100 g skein)

NEEDLES
❦ US 7/4.5 mm 24"/60 cm or longer circular needle
❦ US 9/5.5 mm 24"/60 cm or longer circular needle
Adjust needle size if necessary to obtain correct gauge.

NOTIONS
❦ Spare circular needle or waste yarn
❦ Tapestry needle
❦ Small piece of felt that matches color of yarn
❦ Sewing needle and thread
❦ Pin back or small stitch holder

GAUGE
Using larger needle, 16 sts and 22 rows in St st =
4"/10 cm square, blocked

PATTERN NOTE
❦ The scarf is worked sideways in two pieces from the
edges inward; the two pieces are joined in the
center using 3-needle bind-off (see page 134 for a
photo tutorial).

SPECIAL STITCHES
Central double decrease (cdd): Sl 2 sts as if to knit 2
together, knit 1, pass slipped sts over—2 sts dec'd.
Double yarnover (2yo): Wrap yarn around LH needle
twice; on next row, drop first yo to make a single
elongated yo.

Scarf

First Half
With larger needle, CO 321 sts.
Rows 1, 3, & 5 (WS): K2, *k2, p5; rep from * to last 4
sts, k4.
Rows 2 & 4 (RS): P4, *k5, p2; rep from * to last 2 sts,
p2.
Row 6: P2, *p2, ssk, k3; rep from * to last 4 sts, p4—
276 sts.
Rows 7 & 9: Work sts as they present themselves.
Row 8: P2, *p2, k2, k2tog; rep from * to last 4 sts, p4—
231 sts.
Row 10: P2, *p2, cdd; rep from * to last 4 sts, p4—141
sts.
Change to smaller needle.
Rows 11–15: Knit.
Row 16: Kf&b to end—282 sts.
Change to larger needle.
Rows 17–23: Work in St st.
Change to smaller needle.
Row 24: K2tog to end—141 sts.
Rows 25–27: Knit.
Cut yarn. Transfer sts to spare circular needle or waste
yarn and set aside.

Second Half
Work same as for the First Half, ending on Row 25. Do
not cut yarn.

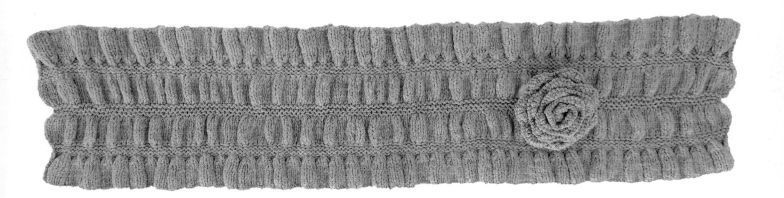

Other options for wearing Shirring Cowl.

Finishing

Using smaller needle as the third needle and yarn from Second Half, with RS facing each other, join First and Second Halves using 3-needle BO.

Weave in ends. Block lightly, being careful to not stretch the ruching.

Rose

Using larger needle, CO 211 sts.

Row 1 (WS): Purl.

Row 2 (RS): K2; [k1 then pass st just worked back to LH needle; use RH needle to lift next 8 sts 1 at a time over this st and off needle; 2yo, then knit the first st again, k2] 19 times.

Row 3: P1, [p2tog, (k1, p1, k1, p1, k1) into 2yo, p1] 19 times, p1—135 sts.

Row 4: Knit.

BO all sts purlwise.

Shape Rose as follows: Lay the fabric on flat surface with WS facing up. Coil the piece and tack the BO edges tog as you go to secure the rolled fabric. The bottom (sewn BO edge) will have the RS facing out and the WS of the CO edge will curl outward to form rose petals.

Sew Rose onto a round piece of felt using whipstitch and attach pin back or a small stitch holder. *Note: Using a stitch holder as a scarf pin allows you to secure several layers of scarf at once.*

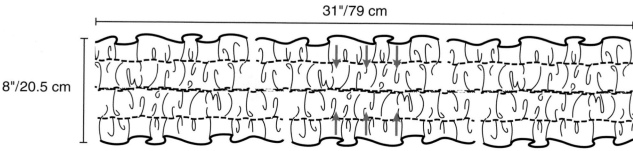

31"/79 cm

8"/20.5 cm

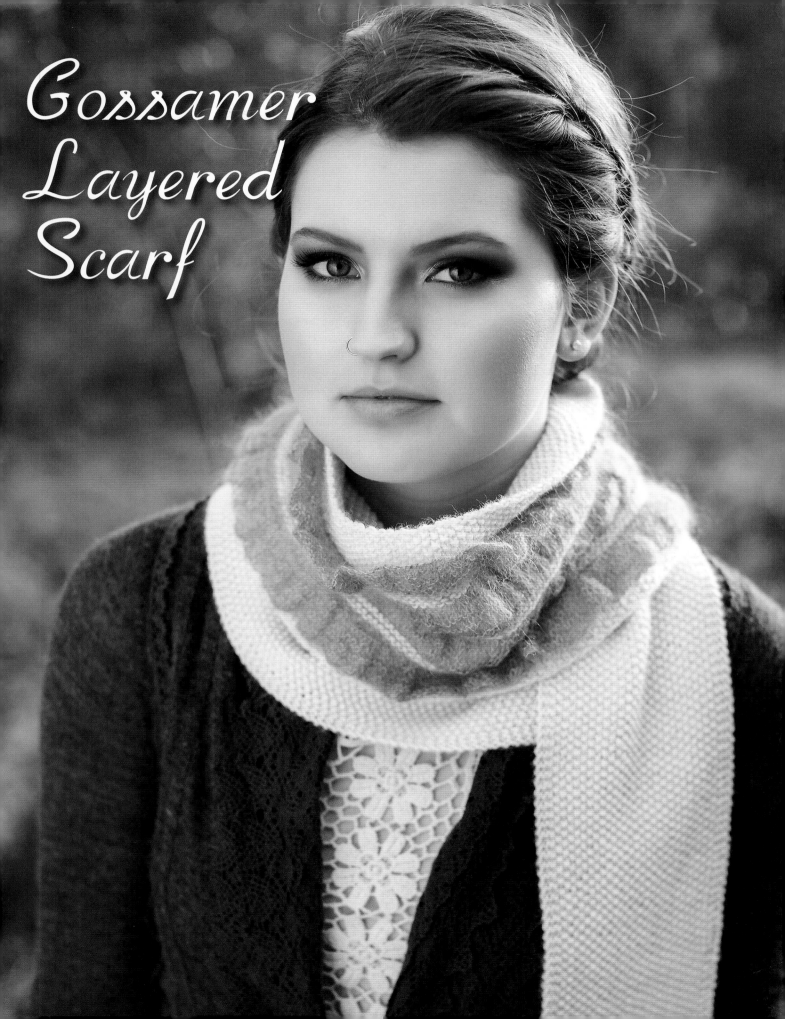

Gossamer Layered Scarf

FINISHED MEASUREMENTS

6½"/16.5 cm wide and 69½"/176.5 cm long

YARN

Color A: 385 yds/352 m DK weight #3 yarn (shown in #2004 Ivory, Shibui Knits Baby Alpaca; 100% baby alpaca; 255 yds/233 m per 100 g skein)

Color B: 233 yds/213 m lace weight #0 yarn (shown in #2010 Flaxen, Shibui Knits Silk Cloud; 60% kid mohair, 40% silk; 330 yds/300 m per 25 g skein)

NEEDLES

❀ US 4/3.5 mm 24"/60 cm or longer circular needle
❀ US 5/3.75 mm 24"/60 cm or longer circular needle
❀ Two US 6/4 mm 24"/60 cm or longer circular needles
❀ US 8/5 mm 24"/60 cm or longer circular needle

Adjust all needle sizes (up or down) as necessary to obtain correct gauge.

NOTIONS

❀ Locking stitch markers in 2 colors (A and B)
❀ Stitch holder
❀ Tapestry needle

GAUGE

Using A and US 5/3.75 mm needles, 28 sts and 40 rows in Seed st = 4"/10 cm square, blocked

PATTERN NOTES

❀ Changes in needle sizes used to create wider fabric for ruching.

❀ Center Section is comprised of two identical halves that are joined in the center using 3-needle BO (see page 134 for a photo tutorial).

❀ Both Center Section halves have two layers of fabric: an underlayer (Layer 1) that is worked in Seed st with A and a top layer (Layer 2) that has a ruffle and a ruched stripe, both worked with B.

❀ After the Center Section is complete, stitches are picked up along each side and then worked down to create ties that have angled ends shaped with short rows (see page 135 for a photo tutorial).

❀ See page 133 for a photo tutorial for 3-needle join.

PATTERN STITCH
Seed Stitch (odd number of sts)
Patt row: *K1, p1; rep from * to last st, k1.
Rep Patt row on RS and WS rows for patt.

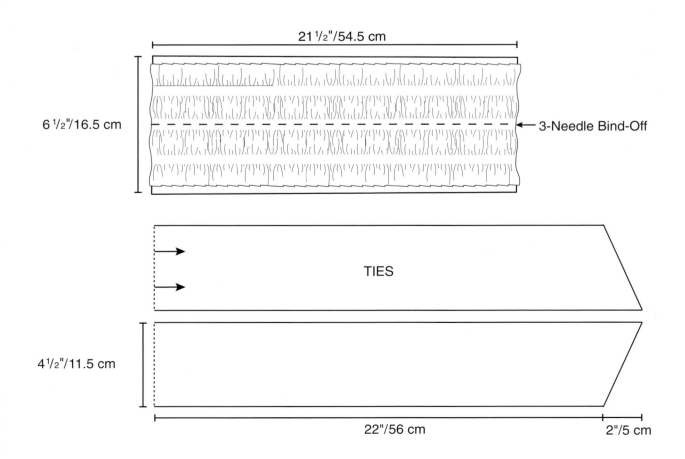

21½"/54.5 cm

6½"/16.5 cm

← 3-Needle Bind-Off

TIES

4½"/11.5 cm

22"/56 cm

2"/5 cm

Center Section

Side One

Layer 1

With A and US 8/5 mm needles, CO 133 sts.
Change to US 6/4 mm needles.
Rows 1 (WS)–7: Work in Seed st, and on last row, place marker A in first st and marker B in last st.
Rows 8–15: Work in Seed st.
Set aside; do not cut A.

Layer 2 (Ruffle)

With B and US 8/5 mm needles, CO 266 sts.
Rows 1 (RS)–4: Knit.
Change to US 6/4 mm needles.
Row 5: Knit.
Row 6: *K2tog, k2; rep from * to last 2 sts, k2tog—199 sts.
Rows 7–9: Knit.
Change to US 5/3.75 mm needles.
Row 10: K1, *k2tog, k1; rep from * to end—133 sts. Do not cut B.

Join Layers

Joining row (RS): With RS of both facing, holding Layer 2 in front of Layer 1 and using US 5/3.75 mm needle and BOTH A and B held tog, join layers using 3-needle join.
Using A and B held tog, knit 4 rows.

Separate Layers

With RS facing, separate the A and B sts onto 2 needles as follows: Layer 1 (A) on back needle (US 4/3.5 mm) and Layer 2 (B) on front needle (US 5/3.75 mm)—133 sts on each needle.

Layer 1

Turn so that Layer 1 has WS facing.
Using US 6/4 mm needles and A, work 14 rows in Seed st.
Transfer sts to US 4/3.5 mm needle for holder. Do not cut A.

Layer 2 (Ruche)

With WS facing, using US 5/3.75 needles and B, work
as follows:

Row 1 (WS): K2, *kf&b; rep from * last 2 sts, k2—262
sts.

Row 2 (RS): Knit.

Change to US 6/4 mm needles.

Rows 3–4: Knit.

Change to US 8/5 mm needles.

Rows 5–6: Knit.

Change to US 6/4 mm needles.

Rows 7–8: Knit.

Change to US 5/3.75 mm needles.

Row 9: Knit.

Row 10: K2, *k2tog; rep from * to last 2 sts, k2—133
sts. Do not cut B.

Center Section Join

Joining row (WS): With WS facing, holding Layer 1 in
front of Layer 2 and using US 5/3.75 mm needle and
BOTH A and B held tog, join layers using 3-needle
join.

Put sts on st holder or scrap yarn. Cut yarns.

Side Two

Rep instructions for Side One. Leave sts on needle; do
not cut yarn.

Join Side One and Side Two

Transfer Side One sts to US 4/3.5 mm needle.

With RS of Side One facing RS of Side Two, using US
8/5 mm needle and A and B held tog, join Side One
to Side Two using 3-needle BO.

Ties

*Note: When there are two layers, all sts are picked up
in Layer 1 only.*

Pick-up row (RS): With RS of one short edge facing,
using US 5/3.75 mm needle and A, pick up and knit
33 sts between markers A and B along Layer 1—33
sts.

Set-up row (WS): K3, work in Seed st to last 3 sts, k3.

Patterns are now established: 3 selvedge sts on each
side worked in Garter st and Seed st between the
selvedge sts.

First Tie

Work in patt until tie meas 20"/51 cm or desired
length, ending on a WS row.

Maintaining patt, shape ends with short rows as follows:

Short Row Set 1: *(RS)* Work 30 sts, w&t; *(WS)* work to
end of row.

Short Row Set 2: Work 27 sts, w&t; work to end of row.

Short Row Set 3: Work 24 sts, w&t; work to end of row.

Short Row Set 4: Work 21 sts, w&t; work to end of row.

Short Row Set 5: Work 18 sts, w&t; work to end of row.

Short Row Set 6: Work 15 sts, w&t; work to end of row.

Short Row Set 7: Work 12 sts, w&t; work to end of row.

Short Row Set 8: Work 9 sts, w&t; work to end of row.

Short Row Set 9: Work 6 sts, w&t; work to end of row.

Short Row Set 10: Work 3 sts, w&t; work to end of row.

Other ways to wear your Gossamer Layered Scarf.

Next row (RS): Work across entire row, hiding wraps when you come to them.

Knit 3 rows.

BO loosely.

Second Tie

Rep Pick-up row on other side and work as for first tie until tie meas 20"/51 cm or desired length, ending on a RS row.

Maintaining patt, shape ends with short rows as follows:

Short Row Set 1: *(WS)* Work 30 sts, w&t; *(RS)* work to end of row.

Short Row Set 2: Work 27 sts, w&t; work to end of row.

Short Row Set 3: Work 24 sts, w&t; work to end of row.

Short Row Set 4: Work 21 sts, w&t; work to end of row.

Short Row Set 5: Work 18 sts, w&t; work to end of row.

Short Row Set 6: Work 15 sts, w&t; work to end of row.

Short Row Set 7: Work 12 sts, w&t; work to end of row.

Short Row Set 8: Work 9 sts, w&t; work to end of row.

Short Row Set 9: Work 6 sts, w&t; work to end of row.

Short Row Set 10: Work 3 sts, w&t; work to end of row.

Next row (WS): Work across entire row, hiding wraps when you come to them.

Knit 3 rows.

BO loosely.

Finishing

Weave in ends and block flat as follows: Gently shape Center Section—do not stretch, or ruffled and ruched section will flatten out. Stretch ties to measurement on schematic.

A Study in Lace

I really like the look of lace worked in a chunky-weight yarn—the juxtaposition of its delicate patterning done in a yarn rigid enough to show all of the intricate detail. Both these pieces highlight this design element.

Sweetheart Cowl

The Sweetheart Cowl is worked in the round, so every round is knit on the right side. The turned-under picot edges make for a sweet, tiny scalloped border at both the top and bottom of the cowl. As far as lace is concerned, this is a simple, straightforward pattern to follow on a basic eight-stitch repeat.

Chantilly Ascot

The Chantilly Ascot, however, is not for the beginner lace knitter. It has a very pronounced twisted-stitch lace pattern that is interesting and complex. It is knit flat, and includes purl-through-the-back-loop stitches on wrong side rows. If you can navigate through this complex lace pattern that I found in a Japanese stitch dictionary, you will be richly rewarded with a beautiful, truly one-of-a-kind piece that you can wear dressed up or down for warmth.

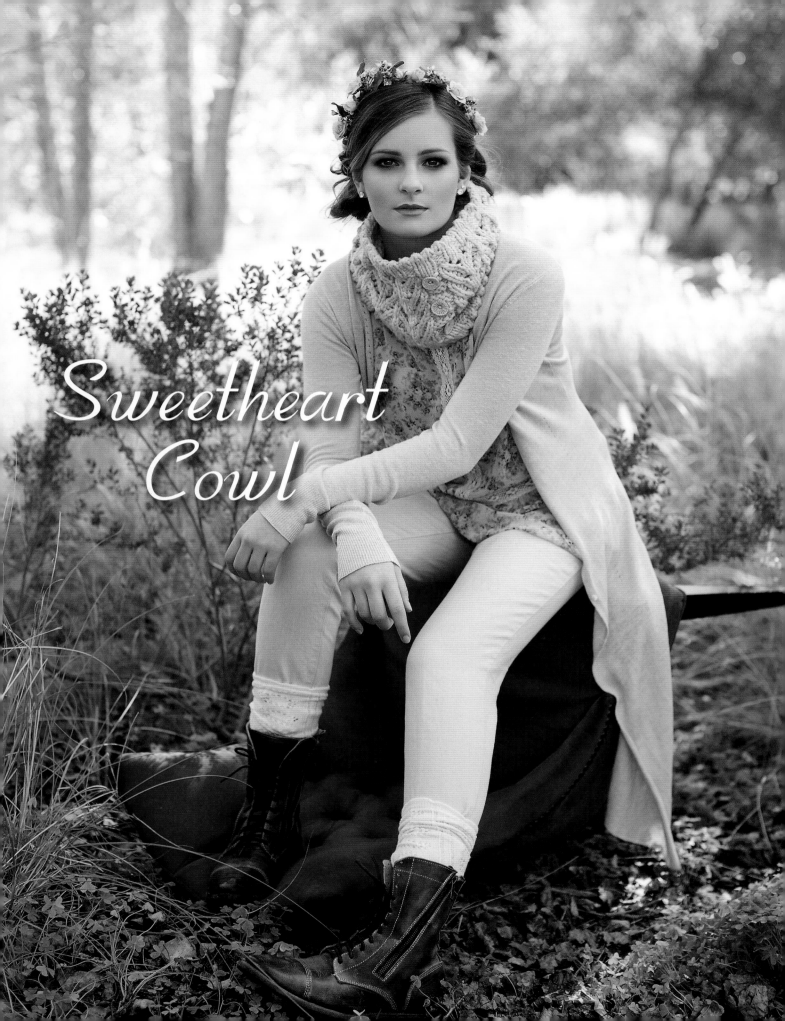

Sweetheart Cowl

FINISHED MEASUREMENTS
8"/20.5 cm tall and 25½"/65 cm circumference at base

YARN
120 yds/110 m chunky weight #5 yarn (shown in Sunkissed, Spud & Chloë Outer; 65% wool, 35% organic cotton; 60 yds/55 m per 100 g skein)

NEEDLES
❀ US 10½/6.5 mm 24"/60 cm circular needle
Adjust needle size if necessary to obtain correct gauge.

NOTIONS
❀ Stitch markers
❀ Tapestry needle
❀ Three 1"/2.5 cm buttons

GAUGE
14 sts and 20 rnds in Lace patt = 4"/10 cm square, blocked
12 sts and 20 rnds in St st = 4"/10 cm square, blocked

PATTERN NOTES
❀ The cowl is knit in one piece in the round from the bottom up.

SPECIAL STITCHES
Central double decrease (cdd): Sl 2 sts as if to knit 2 together, knit 1, pass slipped sts over—2 sts dec'd.

PATTERN STITCHES

Center Pattern (5 sts)
Rnd 1: P1, k3, p1.
Rnds 2–3: P5.
Rnd 4: P1, k3, p1.
Rep Rnds 1–4 for patt.

Lace Pattern (multiple of 8 sts + 9)
Note: A chart is also provided.
Rnds 1–2: K1, *yo, k1, k2tog, k1, ssk, k1, yo, k1; rep from * to end.
Rnd 3: K1, *k1, k2tog, yo, k1, yo, ssk, k2; rep from * to end.
Rnd 4: K1, *k2tog, yo, k3, yo, ssk, k1; rep from * to end.
Rnd 5: K2tog, *yo, k5, yo, cdd; rep from * to last 7 sts, yo, k5, yo, ssk.
Rep Rnds 1–5 for patt.

KEY

□	Knit
⋀	Central double decrease
○	Yo
＼	Ssk
／	K2tog
□	8-st pat rep

LACE PATTERN

Cowl

Picot Edge and Rib

CO 86 sts. Mark beg of rnd and join, taking care not to twist sts.

Knit 1 rnd.

Eyelet rnd: *Yo, k2tog; rep from * to end.

Rnds 1–2: Knit.

Rnds 3–6: P1, k3, p2, k3, [p2, k2, p1, k2, p1] 9 times, p1, k3, p1.

Body

Set-up rnd: P1, k3, p1, knit to end.

Rnd 1: Working Rnd 1 of each patt, work Center patt over 5 sts, work Lace patt to end.

Rnds 2–20: Cont working patts, ending having worked 5 reps of Center patt and 4 reps of Lace patt.

Rnds 21–24: Work Rnds 1–4 of patts.

Dec rnd: P1, k3, p1, k2tog, k2, *k3, cdd, k2; rep from * to last 5 sts, k3, ssk—66 sts.

Rib and Picot Edge

Rnds 1–4: P1, k3, p2, k2, [p2, k3, p1] 9 times, p1, k2, p1.

Rnds 5–6: Knit.

Eyelet rnd: *Yo, k2tog; rep from * to end.

Knit 1 rnd.

BO.

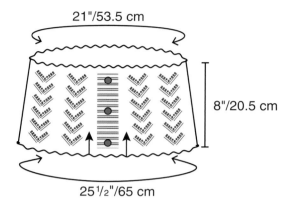

21"/53.5 cm

8"/20.5 cm

25½"/65 cm

Finishing

Fold both edges toward WS at Eyelet rnds to form picot edges and sew in place very loosely to retain elasticity, especially along the top edge.

Weave in ends. Block to shape. Sew buttons in place, referring to schematic for placement.

Chantilly
Ascot

FINISHED MEASUREMENTS
7½"/19 cm wide and 36"/91.5 cm long

YARN
220 yds/201 m worsted weight #4 yarn (shown in
Lagoon, Blue Sky Alpacas Worsted Hand Dyes; 50%
royal alpaca, 50% merino wool; 100 yds/91 m per
110 g skein)

NEEDLES
❧ Set of US 8/5 mm straight knitting needles
❧ 2 sets of US 9/5.5 mm straight knitting needles
*Adjust both needle sizes (up or down) if necessary to
obtain correct gauge.*

NOTIONS
❧ Stitch holder
❧ Locking stitch markers
❧ Tapestry needle

GAUGE
Using smaller needles, 22 sts and 28 rows in Body patt
= 4"/10 cm square, blocked

PATTERN NOTES
❧ Scarf is worked in two halves from the bottom of
lace section to the center back; these halves are
joined together using 3-needle BO (see page 134 for
a photo tutorial).
❧ Slip first stitch of every row purlwise with yarn held
to right side, i.e., with yarn held in front on RS rows
and with yarn held in back on WS rows.

SPECIAL STITCHES
Twisted right-slanting dec (k2tog-T): Sl 1 purlwise,
sl 1 knitwise, return 2 sts to LH needle, k2tog—1 st
dec'd.
Twisted left-slanting dec (skp-T): Sl 1 purlwise, k1,
psso—1 st dec'd.
Twisted right-slanting double dec (k3tog-T): Sl 2
purlwise, sl 1 knitwise, return 3 sts to LH needle,
k3tog—2 sts dec'd.
Twisted left-slanting double dec (sk2p-T): Sl 1 purlwise, k2tog, psso—2 sts dec'd.

PATTERN STITCH

Lace Pattern (worked over 33 sts)

Note: A chart is also provided.

Row 1 (RS): Sl 1 wyif, k1-tbl, p1, [yo, ssk] twice, p3, k2tog-T, [p1, k1-tbl] twice, yo, p1, yo, [k1-tbl, p1] twice, skp-T, p3, [k2tog, yo] twice, p1, k1-tbl, k1.

Row 2 (WS): Sl 1 wyib, p1-tbl, k1, p4, k3, [p1-tbl, k1] twice, p1-tbl, p1, k1, p1, [p1-tbl, k1] twice, p1-tbl, k3, p4, k1, p1-tbl, p1.

Row 3: Sl 1, k1-tbl, p1, k1, [yo, ssk] twice, p1, k2tog-T, p1, [k1-tbl, p1, k1-tbl, yo] twice, [k1-tbl, p1] twice, skp-T, p1, [k2tog, yo] twice, k1, p1, k1-tbl, k1.

Row 4: Sl1, p1-tbl, k1, p5, [k1, p1-tbl] 8 times, k1, p5, k1, p1-tbl, p1.

Row 5: Sl 1, k1-tbl, p1, [yo, ssk] twice, yo, k3tog-T, [p1, k1-tbl] twice, yo, [p1, k1-tbl] twice, p1, yo, [k1-tbl, p1] twice, sk2p-T, [yo, k2tog] twice, yo, p1, k1-tbl, k1.

Row 6: Sl 1, p1-tbl, k1, p5, [p1-tbl, k1] twice, p1-tbl, p1, [k1, p1-tbl] twice, k1, p1, [p1-tbl, k1] twice, p1-tbl, p5, k1, p1-tbl, p1.

Row 7: Sl 1, k1-tbl, p1, k1, yo, ssk, yo, k3tog-T, ([p1, k1-tbl] twice, yo, k1-tbl, p1, k1-tbl) twice, p1, sk2p-T, yo, k2tog, yo, k1, p1, k1-tbl, k1.

Row 8: Sl 1, p1-tbl, k1, p4, [p1-tbl, k1] 9 times, p1-tbl, p4, k1, p1-tbl, p1.

Row 9: Sl 1, k1-tbl, p1, yo, ssk, yo, k3tog-T, [p1, k1-tbl] twice, yo, [p1, k1-tbl] 4 times, p1, yo, [k1-tbl, p1] twice, sk2p-T, yo, k2tog, yo, p1, k1-tbl, k1.

Row 10: Sl 1, p1-tbl, k1, p3, [p1-tbl, k1] twice, p1-tbl, p1, [k1, p1-tbl] 4 times, k1, p1, [p1-tbl, k1] twice, p1-tbl, p3, k1, p1-tbl, p1.

Row 11: Sl 1, k1-tbl, p1, k1, yo, k3tog-T, [p1, k1-tbl] twice, yo, [k1-tbl, p1] 5 times, k1-tbl, yo, [k1-tbl, p1] twice, sk2p-T, yo, k1, p1, k1-tbl, k1.

Row 12: Sl 1, p1-tbl, k1, p2, [p1-tbl, k1] 11 times, p1-tbl, p2, k1, p1-tbl, p1.

Row 13: Sl 1, k1-tbl, p1, yo, k3tog-T, [p1, k1-tbl] twice, yo, [p1, k1-tbl] 6 times, p1, yo, [k1-tbl, p1] twice, sk2p-T, yo, p1, k1-tbl, k1.

Row 14: Sl 1, p1-tbl, k1, p1, [p1-tbl, k1] twice, p1-tbl, p1, [k1, p1-tbl] 6 times, k1, p1, p1-tbl, k1, p1-tbl, [k1, p1-tbl, p1] twice.

Row 15: Sl 1, k1-tbl, p1, k2tog-T, [p1, k1-tbl] twice, yo, [k1-tbl, p1] 7 times, k1-tbl, yo, [k1-tbl, p1] twice, skp-T, p1, k1-tbl, k1.

Row 16: Sl 1, [p1-tbl, k1] 15 times, p1-tbl, p1.

Rep Rows 1–16 for patt.

First Half

With smaller needles, CO 33 sts.

Knit 3 rows.

Change to larger needles.

Rows 1 (RS)–32: Work Rows 1–16 of Lace patt twice.

Rows 33–42: Work Rows 1–10 of Lace patt.

Divide sts for slit: With RS facing and other set of larger needles held parallel, *sl 1 to front needle, sl 1 to back needle; rep from * to last st, sl 1 to front

LACE PATTERN

KEY

☐	RS: Knit / WS: Purl
•	RS: Purl / WS: Knit
V	Sl 1 with yarn held to RS
Ϙ	RS: K1-tbl / WS: P1-tbl
O	Yo
\	Ssk
/	K2tog
⌐	K2tog-T
⌐	Skp-T
⋇	K3tog-T
⋇	Sk2p-T

needle—17 sts on front needle, 16 sts on back needle.

Slit Front
Worked over 17 sts on front needle.
Row 1 (RS): Using larger needles, sl 1, k1-tbl, [p1, k1-tbl] 7 times, k1.
Row 2 (WS): Sl 1, p1-tbl, [k1, p1-tbl] 7 times, p1.
Rep [Rows 1–2] 6 more times. Do not cut yarn.

Slit Back
Worked over 16 sts on back needle.
With WS facing, join new yarn.
Inc row (WS): Using larger needles, sl 1, [k1-tbl, p1] 7 times, M1, k1—17 sts.
Row 1 (RS): Sl 1, p1-tbl, [k1, p1-tbl] 7 times, p1.
Row 2: Sl 1, [k1-tbl, p1] 7 times, k1-tbl, k1.
Rep [Rows 1–2] 5 more times, then rep Row 1 once. Cut yarn.
Join slit top: With RS facing, join sts onto 1 smaller needle as follows: *Sl 1 from front needle to smaller needle, sl 1 from back needle to smaller needle; rep from * to end—34 sts.

Body
Note: A chart is also provided.
With RS facing and using smaller needles and yarn from Slit Front, work as follows:

Row 1 (RS): Sl 1, k1-tbl, p1, *k1-tbl, k1, p1-tbl, p1; rep from * to last 3 sts, k1-tbl, M1, k1-tbl, k1—35 sts.
Row 2 (WS): Sl 1, p1-tbl, k1, M1P, p1-tbl, p1, *k1-tbl, k1, p1-tbl, p1; rep from * to last 2 sts, M1P, p1-tbl, p1—37 sts.
Row 3: Sl 1, k1-tbl, p1, M1, *p1, k1-tbl, k1, p1-tbl; rep from * to last 6 sts, p1, k1-tbl, M1, [k1-tbl, k1] twice—39 sts.
Row 4: Sl 1, p1-tbl, k1, p1-tbl, p1, M1P, p1-tbl, p1; *k1-tbl, k1, p1-tbl, p1; rep from * to last 4 sts, M1P, [p1-tbl, p1] twice—41 sts.
Row 5: Sl 1, k1-tbl, p1, k1-tbl, k1, M1, *p1, k1-tbl, k1, p1-tbl; rep from * to last 8 sts, p1, k1-tbl, M1, p1-tbl, p1, [k1-tbl, k1] twice—43 sts.
Row 6: Sl 1, p1-tbl, k1, p1-tbl, *p1, k1-tbl, k1, p1-tbl; rep from * to last 3 sts, p1, p1-tbl, p1.
Row 7: Sl 1, k1-tbl, p1, *k1-tbl, k1, p1-tbl, p1; rep from * to last 4 sts, [k1-tbl, k1] twice.
Rep Rows 6–7 until piece meas 9"/23 cm from top of slit, ending with a WS row.
Place sts on holder or scrap yarn. Cut yarn.

Second Half
With smaller needles, CO 33 sts.
Knit 3 rows.
Change to larger needles.
Rows 1 (RS)–32: Work Rows 1–16 of Lace patt twice.
Rows 33–42: Work Rows 1–10 of Lace patt.

BODY PATTERN

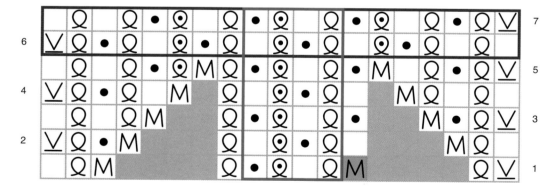

KEY

☐	RS: Knit / WS: Purl
•	RS: Purl / WS: Knit
V	Sl 1 with yarn held to RS
℧	RS: K1-tbl / WS: P1-tbl
☺	RS: P1-tbl / WS: K1-tbl
M	RS: M1 / WS: M1P
M	First Half: P1 / Second Half: M1
▨	No stitch
☐	4-st rep
☐	2-row rep

Body

Change to smaller needles.

Row 1 (RS): Sl 1, k1-tbl, M1, *p1, k1-tbl, k1, p1-tbl; rep from * to last 3 sts, k1-tbl, M1, k1-tbl, k1—35 sts.

Rows 2 (WS)–7: Rep Rows 2–7 of First Half Body—43 sts.

Rep Rows 6–7 of First Half Body until Second Half Body meas 10"/25.5 cm, ending with a WS row.

Transfer sts to larger needle. Do not cut yarn.

Finishing

Transfer First Half Body to larger needle.

Using larger needle, with RS facing each other, join both sides tog using 3-needle BO.

Weave in ends. Block body lightly to shape; block lace ends firmly to open up patt.

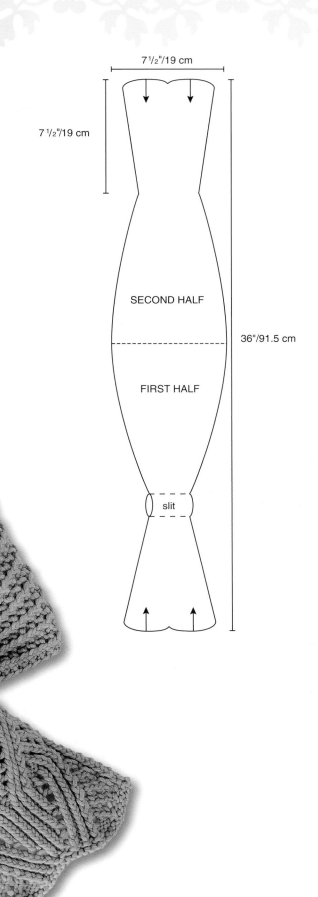

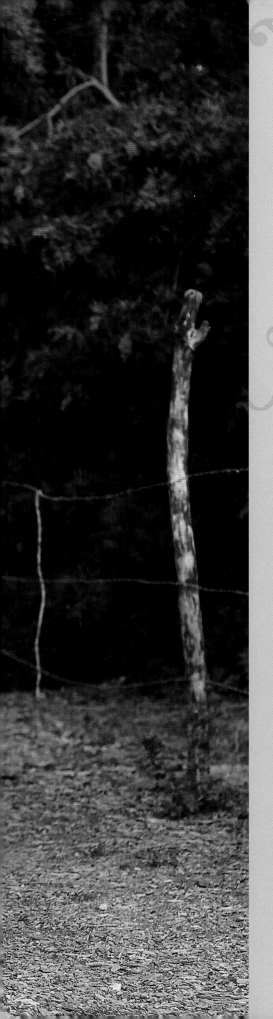

Distinctive Denim Knits

For these two designs, I wanted to incorporate the look of distressed denim. Madelinetosh yarn has such depth and layering of color that even a single hue of blue can take on the feel of well-worn denim fabric. The yarn used for both of these projects is single-ply worsted-weight wool, which is probably my favorite yarn to knit with. It has incredible stitch definition, but is also soft to the touch, with just a slight halo without being too fuzzy.

These two scarves not only have the same type of yarn in common, but also include what I call "design blocking": the incorporation of a "block" of pattern surrounded by sections that are solid-knit or subtly patterned. Design blocking allows the details of the inset to pop by contrast and also relieves the knitter of having to carry out intricate colorwork or stitch patterning over the entirety of a project.

Ricrac Cowl

The Ricrac Cowl is perfect for the knitter new to working with multiple colors in a project. It utilizes a slip-stitch color pattern, so only one color is worked at a time, but has the appearance of a pattern done with Fair Isle technique. Also, more than half of the scarf is done in 2x2 rib, so the confined color section makes the project very manageable. Because it is knitted in the round, you are always stranding your yarn on the back side of the work, which allows for more consistent tension. I like a folded cowl because it looks and feels cozier than a single layer. I also added an optional leather toggle, so as to really draw the cowl in around your neck, or you can leave it undone and draped.

Diamonds & Lace Convertible Scarf

The Diamonds & Lace Convertible Scarf is also a design block scarf that includes diamond patterns done with two different techniques. In the center there is an open-lace diamond stitch pattern; the blocks on either side have more subtle diamonds formed by purl stitches worked against a background of stockinette stitch. This versatile scarf converts to an infinity loop by buttoning the ends together with the tiny open-work faux-cable buttonholes.

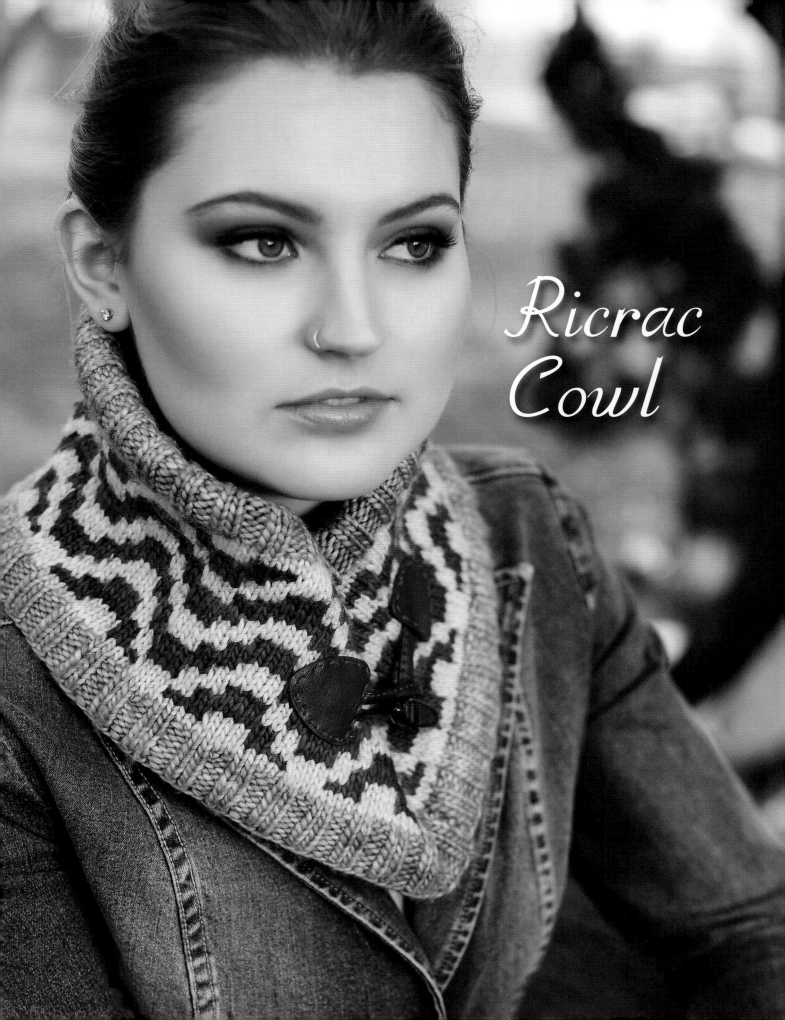

Ricrac
Cowl

FINISHED MEASUREMENTS

11½"/29 cm tall and 27½"/70 cm circumference

YARN

Color A: 200 yds/183 m worsted weight #4 yarn (shown in Well Water, Madelinetosh Tosh Merino; 100% superwash merino wool; 210 yds/192 m per 100 g skein)

Color B: 56 yds/51 m worsted weight #4 yarn (shown in Tart, Madelinetosh Tosh Merino; 100% superwash merino wool; 210 yds/192 m per 100 g skein)

Color C: 65 yds/59.5 m worsted weight #4 yarn (shown in Paper, Madelinetosh Tosh Merino; 100% superwash merino wool; 210 yds/192 m per 100 g skein)

NEEDLES

❖ US 7/4.5 mm 24"/60 cm circular needle

Adjust needle size (up or down) if necessary to obtain correct gauge.

NOTIONS

❖ Stitch marker

❖ Tapestry needle

❖ 5"/12.5 cm leather toggle closure

GAUGE

23 sts and 46 rnds in Slipped Stitch Wave patt = 4"/10 cm square, blocked

24 sts and 29 rnds in 2x2 Rib = 4"/10 cm square, lightly blocked

PATTERN NOTES

❖ The cowl is knit in one piece in the round.

❖ The color pattern is formed using slipped stitches—only one color is used per round. Carry B and C yarns not in use up inside of cowl; do not cut between stripes.

PATTERN STITCHES

2x2 Rib (multiple of 4 sts)

Patt rnd: *K2, p2; rep from * to end.

Slipped Stitch Wave Pattern (multiple of 16 sts)

Note: A chart is also provided.

Rnds 1–2: With B, sl 2, k4, sl 4, k4, sl 2.

Rnds 3–4: With C, k2, sl 2, k8, sl 2, k2.

Rnds 5–6: With B, k4, [sl 2, k4] twice.

Rnds 7–8: With C, sl 2, k4, sl 4, k4, sl 2.

Rnds 9–10: With B, k2, sl 2, k8, sl 2, k2.

Rnds 11–12: With C, [k4, sl 2] twice, k4.

Rep Rnds 1–12 for patt.

SLIP STITCH WAVE PATTERN

KEY

- ▨ Knit with B
- ☐ Knit with C
- Ⅴ Slip C sts
- ◪ Slip B sts
- ☐ 16-st, 12-rnd rep

Undo the toggle, and you have a completely different look.

Cowl

With A, CO 160 sts. Mark beg of rnd and join, taking
  care not to twist sts.
Work 10 rnds in 2x2 Rib. Cut A.
Join C; knit 2 rnds.
Join B; work Rnds 1–12 of Slipped Stitch Wave patt 3
  times, then rep Rnds 1–2. Cut B.
With C, knit 2 rnds. Cut C.
Join A; knit 1 rnd.
Work in 2x2 Rib until piece meas 11½"/29 cm.
BO loosely in patt.

Finishing

Weave in ends.
Sew leather toggle closure through one layer, referring
  to schematic for placement.
Block lightly to shape.

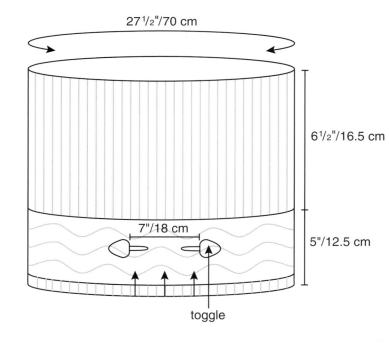

27½"/70 cm

6½"/16.5 cm

7"/18 cm

5"/12.5 cm

toggle

Diamonds & Lace Convertible Scarf

FINISHED MEASUREMENTS

8"/20.5 cm wide and 61½"/156.5 cm long

YARN

Color A: 210 yds/192 m worsted weight #4 yarn (show in Betty Draper's Blue, Madelinetosh Tosh Merino; 100% superwash merino wool; 210 yds/192 m per 100 g skein)

Color B: 147 yds/134.5 m worsted weight #4 yarn (show in Paper, Madelinetosh Tosh Merino; 100% superwash merino wool; 210 yds/192 m per 100 g skein)

NEEDLES

❀ Set of US 7/4.5 mm straight knitting needles
❀ Set of US 8/5 mm straight knitting needles
❀ US H-8/5 mm crochet hook (for provisional cast-on)
Adjust both needle sizes (up or down) if necessary to obtain correct gauge.

NOTIONS

❀ Stitch markers
❀ Tapestry needle
❀ Nine ³⁄₈"/1 cm buttons
❀ Sewing needle and matching thread

GAUGE

Using smaller needles, 23 sts and 24 rows in Diamond patt = 4"/10 cm square, blocked

PATTERN NOTES

❀ Scarf is worked in one piece: The Center Lace Section is worked first and is begun with a provisional CO (see page 132 for a photo tutorial). The scarf continues directly into the Buttonhole Section, which is comprised of a Transition pattern, followed by a Diamond pattern, and ends with a faux cable rib. After the provisional CO is unzipped, the Button Band Section is worked in the opposite direction.

❀ Buttonholes are formed by yo's in the center of the faux cables.

SPECIAL STITCHES

Sk2p: Sl 1 st as if to knit, knit 2 sts together, pass slipped st over—2 sts dec'd.

Cable YO: Pass third st on LH needle over the second and first sts; k1, yo, k1.

Cable M1: Pass third st on LH needle over the second and first sts; k1, M1, k1—1 st inc'd.

PATTERN STITCHES

Note: Charts are also provided for the patterns.

Lace Pattern (worked over 37–45 sts)

Row 1 (RS): K1, [yo, k2tog] twice, yo, k1, ([yo, ssk] twice, yo, sk2p, [yo, k2tog] twice, yo, k1) twice, [yo, ssk] twice, yo, k1—37 sts.

Row 2 and all WS rows: Purl.

Row 3: K1, [yo, k2tog] twice, yo, k2, (k1, [yo, ssk] twice, k1, [k2tog, yo] twice, k2) twice, k1, [yo, ssk] twice, yo, k1—39 sts.

Row 5: K1, [yo, k2tog] 3 times, yo, k1, ([yo, ssk] twice, yo, sk2p, [yo, k2tog] twice, yo, k1) twice, [yo, ssk] 3 times, yo, k1—41 sts.

Row 7: K1, [yo, k2tog] 3 times, yo, k2, (k1, [yo, ssk] twice, k1, [k2tog, yo] twice, k2) twice, k1, [yo, ssk] 3 times, yo, k1—43 sts.

Row 9: K1, [yo, k2tog] 4 times, yo, k1, ([yo, ssk] twice, yo, sk2p, [yo, k2tog] twice, yo, k1) twice, [yo, ssk] 4 times, yo, k1—45 sts.

Row 11: K1, [ssk, yo] 4 times, sk2p, ([yo, k2tog] twice, yo, k1, [yo, ssk] twice, yo, sk2p) twice, [yo, k2tog] 4 times, k1—43 sts.

Row 13: K1, [ssk, yo] 3 times, ssk, k1, ([k2tog, yo] twice, k3, [yo, ssk] twice, k1) twice, [k2tog, yo] 3 times, k2tog, k1—41 sts.

Row 15: K1, [ssk, yo] 3 times, sk2p, ([yo, k2tog] twice, yo, k1, [yo, ssk] twice, yo, sk2p) twice, [yo, k2tog] 3 times, k1—39 sts.

Row 17: K1, [ssk, yo] twice, ssk, k1, ([k2tog, yo] twice, k3, [yo, ssk] twice, k1) twice, [k2tog, yo] twice, k2tog, k1—37 sts.

Row 19: K1, [ssk, yo] twice, sk2p, ([yo, k2tog] twice, yo, k1, [yo, ssk] twice, yo, sk2p) twice, [yo, k2tog] twice, k1—35 sts.

Row 20: Purl.

Rep Rows 1–20 for patt.

Transition Pattern (worked over 36–46 sts)

Row 1 (RS): K1, [yo, k2tog] twice, yo, k1, [k4, p4, k4] twice, k1, [yo, ssk] twice, yo, k1—38 sts.

Row 2 (WS): P7, [p3, k6, p3] twice, p7.

Row 3: K1, [yo, k2tog] twice, yo, k2, ([k2, p3] twice, k2) twice, k2, [yo, ssk] twice, yo, k1—40 sts.

Row 4: P8, [p1, k3, p4, k3, p1] twice, p8.

Row 5: K1, [yo, k2tog] 3 times, yo, k1, [p3, k6, p3] twice, k1, [yo, ssk] 3 times, yo, k1—42 sts.

Row 6: P9, [k3, p6, k3] twice, p9.

Row 7: K1, [yo, k2tog] 3 times, yo, k2, [k1, p3, k4, p3, k1] twice, k2, [yo, ssk] 3 times, yo, k1—44 sts.

Row 8: P10, ([p2, k3] twice, p2) twice, p10.

Row 9: K1, [yo, k2tog] 4 times, yo, k1, [k3, p6, k3] twice, k1, [yo, ssk] 4 times, yo, k1—46 sts.

(continued)

LACE PATTERN

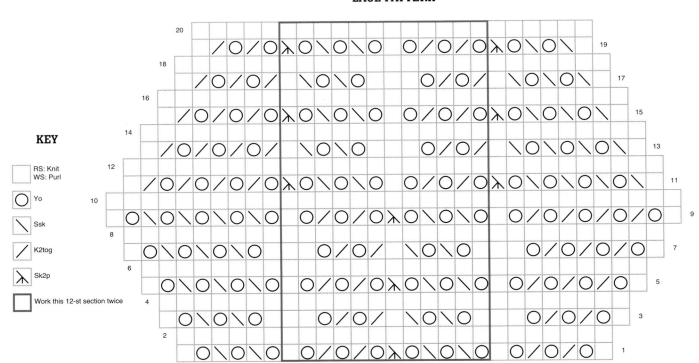

KEY

☐	RS: Knit / WS: Purl
○	Yo
\	Ssk
/	K2tog
⋏	Sk2p
☐	Work this 12-st section twice

Row 10: P11, [p4, k4, p4] twice, p11.

Row 11: K1, [ssk, yo] 4 times, ssk, [k4, p4, k4] twice, [k2tog, yo] 4 times, k2tog, k1—44 sts.

Row 12: P10, [p3, k6, p3] twice, p10.

Row 13: K1, [ssk, yo] 3 times, ssk, k1, ([k2, p3] twice, k2) twice, k1, [k2tog, yo] 3 times, k2tog, k1—42 sts.

Row 14: P9, [p1, k3, p4, k3, p1] twice, p9.

Row 15: K1, [ssk, yo] 3 times, ssk, [p3, k6, p3] twice, [k2tog, yo] 3 times, k2tog, k1—40 sts.

Row 16: P8, [k3, p6, k3] twice, p8.

Row 17: K1, [ssk, yo] twice, ssk, k1, [k1, p3, k4, p3, k1] twice, k1, [k2tog, yo] twice, k2tog, k1—38 sts.

Row 18: P7, ([p2, k3] twice, p2) twice, p7.

Row 19: K1, [ssk, yo] twice, ssk, [k3, p6, k3] twice, [k2tog, yo] twice, k2tog, k1—36 sts.

Row 20: P6, [p4, k4, p4] twice, p6.

Rep Rows 1–20 for patt.

Diamond Pattern (worked over 46 sts)

Row 1 (RS): P7, k4, [k4, p4, k4] twice, k4, p7.

Row 2 (WS): P4, k4, p3, [p3, k6, p3] twice, p3, k4, p4.

Row 3: K6, p3, k2, ([k2, p3] twice, k2) twice, k2, p3, k6.

Row 4: P7, k3, p1, [p1, k3, p4, k3, p1] twice, p1, k3, p7.

Row 5: P3, k5, p3, [p3, k6, p3] twice, p3, k5, p3.

Row 6: K3, p5, k3, [k3, p6, k3] twice, k3, p5, k3.

Row 7: K7, p3, k1, [k1, p3, k4, p3, k1] twice, k1, p3, k7.

Row 8: P6, k3, p2, ([p2, k3] twice, p2) twice, p2, k3, p6.

Row 9: K3, p5, k3, [k3, p6, k3] twice, k3, p5, k3.

Row 10: K7, p4, [p4, k4, p4] twice, p4, k7.

Rep Rows 1–10 for patt.

KEY

- RS: Knit / WS: Purl
- • RS: Purl / WS: Knit
- ○ Yo
- ＼ Ssk
- ／ K2tog
- ⋏ Sk2p
- Work this 12-st section twice.

TRANSITION PATTERN

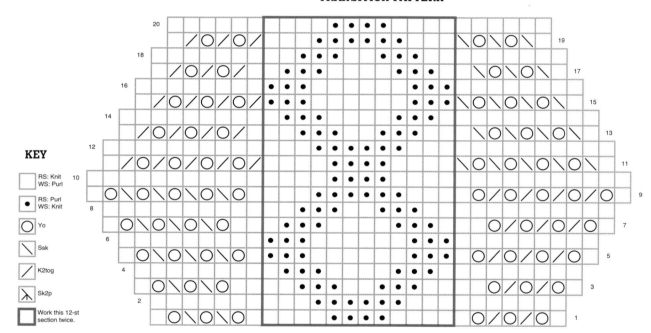

DIAMOND PATTERN

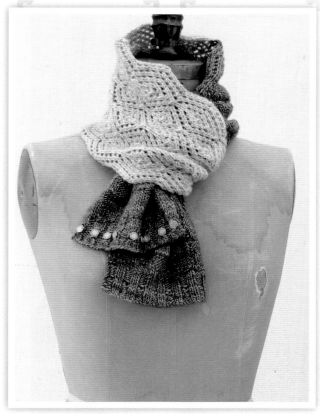

Alternate ways to wear Diamonds & Lace Convertible Scarf.

Scarf

Center Lace Section

Using smaller needles, B, and provisional CO, CO 35 sts.

Work 20-row Lace patt until piece meas approx 28"/71 cm, ending on Row 19.

Buttonhole Section

Cut B, change to larger needles, and join A.

Purl 1 row.

Inc row (RS): K1, [yo, k2tog] twice, yo, k1, [k4, p4, k4] twice, M1, [yo, ssk] twice, yo, k1—38 sts.

Work Rows 2–20 of Transition patt—36 sts.

Work Rows 1–9 of Transition patt—46 sts.

Next row (WS): K7, p4 [p4, k4, p4] twice, p4, k7.

Work Diamond patt until piece meas approx 45"/114.5 cm, ending on Row 10.

Buttonhole Edge

Change to smaller needles.

Row 1 (RS): K3, k2tog, *p2, k3; rep from * to last st, k1—45 sts.

Row 2 and all WS rows: K1, *p3, k2; rep from * to last 4 sts, p3, k1.

Row 3: K4, *p2, k3; rep from * to last st, k1.

Row 5 (Buttonhole row): K1, *Cable YO, p2; rep from * to last 4 sts, Cable YO, k1.

Row 7: Rep Row 3.

Row 9: K1, *Cable M1, p2; rep from * to last 4 sts, Cable M1, k1.

Row 10: Rep Row 2.

BO in patt.

Button Band Section

Unzip provisional CO and place 34 live sts on larger needle. Mark this row.

With WS facing, join A.

Inc row (WS): P5, M1P, purl to end—35 sts.

Inc row (RS): K1, [yo, k2tog] twice, yo, k1, [k4, p4, k4] twice, M1, [yo, ssk] twice, yo, k1—38 sts.

Work Rows 2–20 of Transition patt.

Work Rows 1–9 of Transition patt—46 sts.

Next row (WS): K7, p4 [p4, k4, p4] twice, p4, k7.

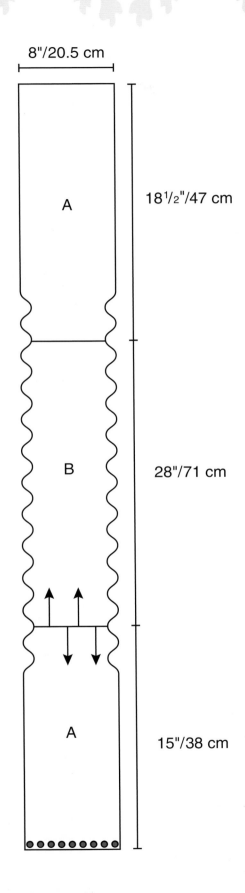

8"/20.5 cm

A

18½"/47 cm

B

28"/71 cm

A

15"/38 cm

Work 10-row Diamond patt until Button Band Section meas approx 13½"/34.5 cm from marked row, ending on Row 10.

Button Band Edge

Change to smaller needles.

Row 1 (RS): K3, k2tog, *p2, k3; rep from * to last st, k1—45 sts.

Row 2 and all WS rows: K1, *p3, k2; rep from * to last 4 sts, p3, k1.

Row 3: K4, *p2, k3; rep from * to last st, k1.

Row 5: K1, *Cable M1, p2; rep from * to last 4 sts, Cable M1, k1.

Rows 7 & 9: Rep Rows 3 & 5.

Row 10: Rep Row 2.

BO in patt.

Finishing

Block to shape, pinning lace firmly to open up.

Sew 9 buttons along Button Band Edge, corresponding to Cable YO buttonholes.

Neck Warmers, Ascot Style

The ascot is one of my favorite shapes for a scarf. I like the way it hugs the neck without being too bulky. I also like how quick an ascot is to knit, using up very little yarn, making it a perfect hand-made gift.

Quilted Lattice Ascot

This is one of my most popular scarf patterns. It's the perfect neck warmer to wear under a coat or jacket. It fits snugly around the back of the neck, providing extra insulation, and has a pretty decorative square that peeks out from the space between the collar or lapels. The body of the ascot is done in Mistake Rib Stitch, a one-row pattern of only knit and purl stitches repeated for every row. I used snap tape to secure this scarf, but the individual snaps sewn on the Snowflake Ascot would work just as well and vice versa. An extra bonus is that this ascot can usually be finished with one skein of most worsted weight yarns, though it does require 15 yards of a contrasting color for the crosshatches of the Quilted Lattice design. But I'm confident most any knitter will be able to dig out from their stash 15 yards of a complementary color in worsted weight that will work!

Snowflake Ascot

The Snowflake Ascot has the same fit and dimensions as the Quilted Lattice Ascot, with the addition of a snowflake design worked in two-color stranded stockinette stitch. Spanning just 33 stitches and 38 rows, the snowflake is a nice size for a first colorwork piece. The body of the scarf has a lot of texture, with cables moving in alternate directions. I chose to leave off any decorative buttons on this piece so as not to interfere with the snowflake design.

Quilted Lattice Ascot

FINISHED MEASUREMENTS
7¹⁄₂"/19 cm wide and 26"/66 cm long

YARN
Color A: 201 yds/184 m worsted weight #4 yarn (shown in Cove, Madelinetosh Tosh Merino; 100% superwash merino wool; 210 yds/192 m per 100 g skein)

Color B: 15 yds/14 m worsted weight #4 yarn (shown in Paper, Madelinetosh Tosh Merino; 100% superwash merino wool; 210 yds/192 m per 100 g skein)

NEEDLES
✿ US 5/3.75 mm circular needle (need to access sts from both ends)
✿ Set of US 6/4 mm straight needles
✿ Set of US 7/4.5 mm straight needles
✿ US 8/5 mm circular needle (need to access sts from both ends)
Adjust all needle sizes (up or down) if necessary to obtain correct gauge.

NOTIONS
✿ Stitch marker
✿ Tapestry needle
✿ Cotton snap tape (2 strips with 3 snaps each)
✿ Three ¹⁄₂"/1.25 cm buttons
✿ Sewing needle and thread

GAUGE
Using US 7/4.5 mm needles, 20 sts and 26 rows in St st = 4"/10 cm square, blocked
Using US 8/5 mm needles, 26 sts and 38 rows in Quilted Lattice patt = 4"/10 cm square, blocked

PATTERN NOTES
✿ Ascot is worked in one piece from end to end.
✿ When slipping multiple stitches, carry the yarn loosely across the fabric.

PATTERN STITCHES

Quilted Lattice (worked over 29 sts)
Row 1 (WS): With B, sl 2 wyif, p1, [sl 5 wyib, k1] 3 times, sl 5 wyib, p1, sl 2 wyif.
Row 2: With A, knit.
Row 3: K2, purl to last 2 sts, k2.
Row 4: With B, sl 5 wyib, * insert RH needle under loose strand and knit next st (bringing st out under strand), sl 5 wyib; rep from * to end.

Row 5: Sl 1 wyif, p1, sl 3 wyib, [k1, sl 5 wyib] 3 times, k1, sl 3 wyib, p1, sl 1 wyif.
Rows 6–7: With A, rep Rows 2–3.
Row 8: With B, sl 2 wyib, k1 under loose strand, *sl 5 wyib, k1 under loose strand; rep from * to last 2 sts, sl 2 wyib.
Rep Rows 1–8 for patt.

Mistake Rib Stitch (odd number of sts)
Patt row: K2, *k2, p2; rep from * to last 5 sts, k2, p1, k2.
Rep Patt row on RS and WS rows for patt.

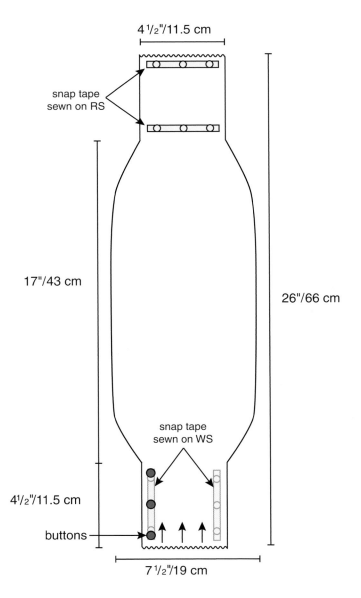

4¹⁄₂"/11.5 cm

snap tape sewn on RS

17"/43 cm

26"/66 cm

snap tape sewn on WS

4¹⁄₂"/11.5 cm

buttons

7¹⁄₂"/19 cm

Quilted Lattice Pattern

When working this pattern, you must pay special attention to which side you are holding the yarn when slipping stitches. WYIB and WYIF refer to the back or front of the work as it faces you, not to the WS and RS of the fabric. If you are on a WS row and slipping WYIB, then the yarn will be held on the back side of your work, which is the RS, and vice versa.

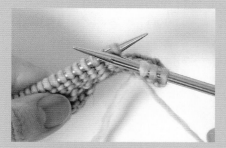

Row 1 (WS): With B on the front side of work (WS), sl 2 sts.

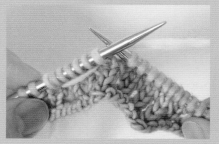

P1 with B, then slip 5 sts with B on the back side of work (RS), p1. This creates a strand that goes across 5 sts on RS.

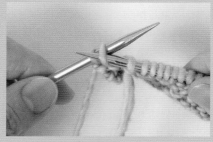

Sl last 2 sts, leaving B on the front side of work (WS).

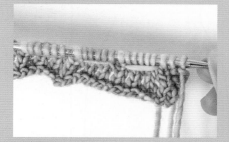

RS of work after Row 1 is complete.

Row 4 (RS): Sl first 5 sts with B in back (WS).

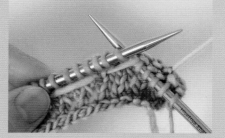

Insert RH needle under loose strand.

Knit next st with B, bringing st out from under strand.

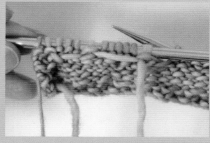

Sl 5 sts with B on the back side of work (WS).

Scarf

First End

With US 5/3.75 mm circular needle and A, CO 30 sts.

Row 1 (RS): Knit.

Row 2 (WS): K1, purl to last st, k1.

Row 3 (Eyelet row): K2tog, *yo, k2tog; rep from * to end—29 sts.

Row 4: K2, purl to last 2 sts, k2.

Row 5: Knit.

Row 6: Rep Row 4. Do not turn.

Slide sts to other end of needle.

Change to US 8/5 mm circular needle. With WS facing, join B. Do not cut A.

Work Rows 1–8 of Quilted Lattice patt.

Work even in Quilted Lattice patt until First End meas 4½"/11.5 cm from Eyelet row, ending on Row 4 of patt. Cut B. Do not turn.

Slide sts to other end of needle.

With RS facing and A, knit 1 row.

Body

Change to US 5/3.75 circular needle.

Next row (WS): K2, purl to last 2 sts, k2.

Inc row (RS): K3, *kf&b 3 times, k1; rep from * to last 2 sts, k2—47 sts.

Work 7 rows in Mistake Rib St patt.

Change to US 6/4 mm needles; work 7 rows in established patt.

Change to US 7/4.5 mm needles; work 7 rows in patt. Mark last row worked.

Change to US 8/5 mm circular needle.

Counting number of rows, work in patt until piece meas 13"/33 cm from Eyelet row, or desired length to center point (see Adjusting the Length of the Scarf). Mark center-point row.

Work same number of rows worked between first marked row to center-point row, ending on a RS row.

Change to US 7/4.5 mm needles. Work 7 rows in patt.

Change to US 6/4 mm needles. Work 7 rows in patt.

Change to US 5/3.75 circular needle. Work 7 rows in patt, ending on a WS row.

Dec row (RS): K3, *k2tog 3 times, k1; rep from * to last 2 sts, k2—29 sts.

Second End

Change to US 8/5 mm circular needle.

Set-up row (WS): K2, purl to last 2 sts, k2. Do not turn.

Slide sts to other end of needle. Do not cut A. With WS facing, join B.

Starting with Row 5, work Quilted Lattice patt until Second End meas 4½"/11.5 cm (or matches First End), ending on Row 8 of patt. Do not turn.

Slide sts back to other end of needle, with RS facing. Cut B.

Next row (RS): With A, knit.

Change to US 5/3.75 circular needle.

Next row (WS): K2, purl to last 2 sts, k2.

Next row: Knit.

Next row (Eyelet row): K2tog, yo, *p2tog, yo; rep from * to last 2 sts, yo, k2tog—29 sts.

Next row: Knit.

Next row: K2, purl to last 2 sts, k2.

BO all sts.

Adjusting the Length of the Scarf

The scarf in the photos is 26"/66 cm long. You can adjust for fit as follows: after reaching center point (13"/33 cm for the scarf shown), try the scarf on for fit. When the Quilted Lattice square is positioned at the base of the front of your neck, the body of the scarf should fit snugly, yet comfortably, with the back of the scarf coming up around the back of your neck high enough to be seen over the collar of a coat. If more length is needed, work more rows until reaching desired center point.

Finishing

Weave in all ends and block lightly.

Fold edges on both ends toward WS at Eyelet row to form picot edges; sew in place with tapestry needle.

With needle and thread, sew cotton snap tape and 3 buttons in place as shown in photo.

Snowflake
Ascot

COLOR PATTERN

KEY

☐	Color A
■	Color B
☐	RS: Knit WS: Purl
•	RS: Purl WS: Knit
╱	K2tog
◯	Yo

FINISHED MEASUREMENTS

6½"/16.5 cm wide (measured at center) and 28"/71 cm long

YARN

Color A: 264 yds (241.5 m) DK weight #3 yarn (shown in #3014 Natural, Manos del Uruguay Silk Blend; 70% merino wool, 30% silk; 150 yds/135 m per 50 g skein)

Color B: 30 yds (27.5 m) DK weight #3 yarn (shown in #3043 Juniper, Manos del Uruguay Silk Blend; 70% merino wool, 30% silk; 150 yds/135 m per 50 g skein)

NEEDLES

⚜ Set of US 2/2.75 mm straight knitting needles (smallest)
⚜ Set of US 4/3.5 mm straight knitting needles (small)
⚜ Set of US 5/3.75 mm straight knitting needles (medium)
⚜ Set of US 6/4 mm straight knitting needles (large)
Adjust all needle sizes if necessary to obtain correct gauge.

NOTIONS

⚜ Locking stitch marker
⚜ Cable needle
⚜ Waste yarn or circular needle
⚜ Tapestry needle
⚜ 6 snaps, size 4

GAUGE

Using large needles, 23 sts and 34 rows in St st = 4"/10 cm square, blocked
Using small needles, 30 sts and 32 rows in 2-color stranded St st = 4"/10 cm square, blocked
Using smallest needles, 30 sts and 36 rows in St st = 4"/10 cm square, blocked
Smallest needles used to achieve same stitch gauge as 2-color stranded section.

PATTERN NOTES

⚜ The scarf is worked in two pieces from the outer edges inward, ending at the center back neck; the two pieces are joined using 3-needle BO (see page 134 for a photo tutorial).
⚜ The colorwork on the ends is worked using 2-color stranded St st.

SPECIAL STITCHES

5/5 LC: Sl 5 sts to cn and hold in front; k5; k5 from cn.
5/5 RC: Sl 5 sts to cn and hold in back; k5; k5 from cn.
3/3 LC Inc: Sl 3 sts to cn and hold in front; k3, M2; k3 from cn—2 sts inc'd.
4/4 RC Inc: Sl 4 sts to cn and hold in back; k4, M2; k4 from cn—2 sts inc'd.
5/5 LC Inc: Sl 5 sts to cn and hold in front; k5, M2; k5 from cn—2 sts inc'd.

PATTERN STITCH

Cable (multiple of 15 sts + 2)
Row 1 (RS): K1, [k5, 5/5 RC] 4 times, k1.
Rows 2–6: Work in St st.
Row 7: K1, [5/5 LC, k5] 4 times, k1.
Rows 8–12: Work in St st.
Rep Rows 1–12 for patt.

Scarf

First Half End

Using small needles and B, CO 33 sts.
Work Color patt chart as follows:
Row 1 (RS): Knit.
Row 2 (WS): K2 (selvedge sts), purl to last 2 sts, k2 (selvedge sts).
Row 3 (Picot row): K2, *yo, k2tog; rep from * to last st, k1.
Row 4: Rep Row 2.
Rows 5–43: Maintaining selvedge sts in Garter st and center 29 sts in St st, complete Color patt chart. Cut B.
Row 44: With A, rep Row 2.

First Half Body

Row 1 (RS): K1, [M1, k6] 5 times, k2—38 sts.
Row 2 (WS): Purl.
Row 3: K1, [3/3 LC Inc, k3] 4 times, k1—46 sts.
Rows 4–8: Work in St st.
Change to medium needles.
Row 9: K1, [k3, 4/4 RC Inc] 4 times, k1—54 sts.
Rows 10–14: Work in St st.
Change to large needles.
Row 15: K1, [5/5 LC Inc, k3] 4 times, k1—62 sts.
Rows 16–20: Work in St st.
Work in Cable patt until Body meas approx 8½"/21.5 cm, ending on Row 3 of Cable patt. Transfer sts to spare circular needle or waste yarn and set aside.

Second Half End

Using small needles and B, CO 33 sts.

Work Rows 1–6 of Color patt chart. Pm in last st and cut B.

Change to smallest needles.

Row 7 (RS): With A, knit.

Row 8 (WS): K2, purl to last 2 sts, k2.

Maintaining selvedge sts in Garter st and center 29 sts in St st, work even until piece meas approx 4"/10 cm from marker, ending on a RS row.

Work Rows 40–43 of Color patt chart. Cut B.

Next row: With A, rep Row 8.

Second Half Body

Work same as for the First Half Body until Body meas approx 9½"/24 cm, ending on Row 9 of Cable patt.

Finishing

Join 2 halves using 3-needle BO. *Note: Sts can also be grafted together.*

Weave in ends.

Fold both ends towards WS at Picot row to form picot edges and sew in place.

Block lightly, being careful to not stretch out cables.

Sew 4 snaps in place, referring to schematic for placement.

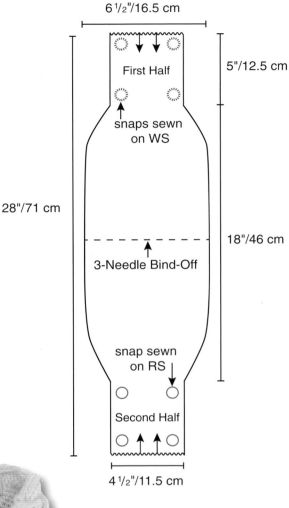

Woolly Bully

The mention of bouclé yarn often summons up images of baby knits or bulky, unflattering sweaters. However, bouclé yarn, when used in a specific way, can look like Sherpa wool, which I'm crazy about. I'm especially fond of the organic feel of the Rowan British Sheep Breeds Bouclé yarn, available in two different gauges, which has the feel and look of freshly shorn sheep.

Fräulein Scarf

The Fräulein Scarf is made with the heavier of the two Rowan yarns and makes for a cozy neck warmer done in the color of the light brown Masham sheep. This simple scarf uses basic increases and decreases to make a ruched center section with ties worked from both ends in a simple but lovely lace pattern. The extra-long ties, which can be wrapped around the neck several times or tied up in a big bow, end in scalloped bottoms.

Gingham & Wool Cowl

The Gingham & Wool Cowl has a slipped stitch country gingham pattern on the front side created by using different shades of Bluefaced Leicester sheep. A Sherpa-like lining on the edges and interior is knit in a finer gauge of the British Sheep Bouclé. The interior and exterior of the cowl are worked on separate layers, folded on either end. The placket is picked up and worked afterwards. Three decorative hooks allow you to wear the cowl tight and buttoned up for extra warmth or open to expose the cozy, sheepish lining within.

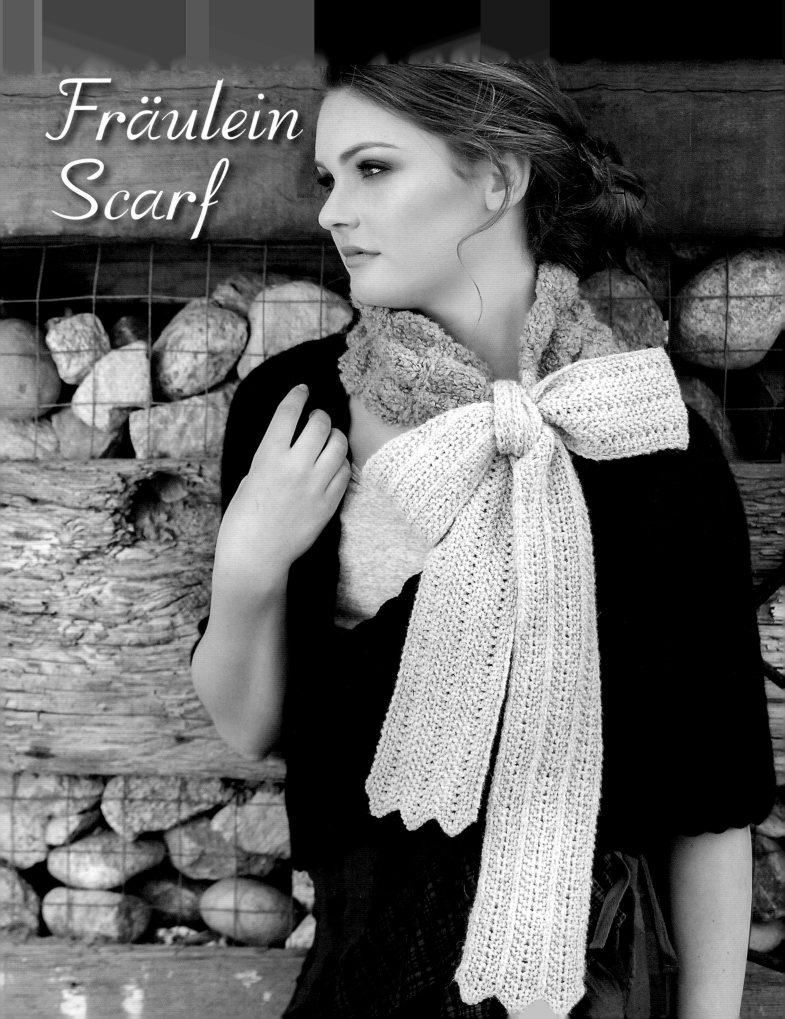

Fräulein
Scarf

FINISHED MEASUREMENTS

5"/12.5 cm wide (at center) and 86"/218.5 cm long, blocked

YARN

Color A: 218 yds/200 m worsted weight #4 yarn (shown in #890 Bolivia, Rowan Lima; 84% baby alpaca, 8% merino wool, 8% nylon; 109 yds/100 m per 50 g skein)

Color B: 66 yds/60 m super bulky weight #6 yarn (shown in #221 Light Brown Masham, Rowan British Sheep Breeds Bouclé; 100% British wool; 66 yds/60 m per 100 g skein)

NEEDLES

* Set of US 7/4.5 mm straight needles (small)
* Set of US 9/5.5 mm straight needles (medium)
* Set of US 11/8 mm straight needles (large)
* US I-9/5.5 mm crochet hook (for provisional CO)

Adjust all needle sizes if necessary to obtain correct gauge.

NOTIONS

* Tapestry needle

GAUGE

Using small needles and A, 37 sts and 28 rows in Lace patt = 4"/10 cm square, blocked

Using large needles and B, $8\frac{1}{2}$ sts and 13 rows in St st = 4"/10 cm square, blocked

PATTERN NOTES

* The center section of the scarf is worked first, starting with a provisional CO (see page 132 for a photo tutorial), then ties are worked out in opposite directions.

SPECIAL STITCHES

Central double decrease (cdd): Sl 2 sts as if to knit 2 together, knit 1, pass slipped sts over—2 sts dec'd.

PATTERN STITCH

Lace Pattern (multiple of 10 sts + 13)

Row 1 (RS): K1, ssk, [k7, cdd] twice, k7, k2tog, k1—27 sts.

Row 2 (WS): K1, [p1, k3, (k1, yo, k1) in next st, k3] 3 times, p1, k1—33 sts.

Rep Rows 1–2 for patt.

Another way to wear the Fräulein Scarf.

First Half

Center Section

Using Provisional CO, with medium needles and B, CO
13 sts.

Inc row (RS): K1, kf&b to last st, k1—24 sts.

Change to large needles.

Rows 1, 3, & 5 (WS): Purl.

Rows 2 & 4 (RS): Knit.

Change to medium needles.

Row 6: K2tog to end—12 sts.

Rows 7–9: Knit.

Row 10: Kf&b to end—24 sts.

Rep Rows 1–10 three more times.

Rep Rows 1–9. Cut B.

Tie

Change to small needles; join A.

Inc row (RS): *Kf&b, [M1, kf&b] 3 times; rep from * to
end—33 sts.

Next row: Knit.

Work Lace patt until tie meas approx 33"/84 cm,
ending on a WS row.

BO knitwise.

Second Half

Unzip provisional CO and transfer 12 live sts to
medium needle; join B with WS facing.

Set-up row (WS): Knit.

Inc row (RS): Kf&b to end—24 sts.

Change to large needles.

Proceed from Row 1 of First Half, Center Section to end
of Tie.

Finishing

Weave in ends. Block to shape.

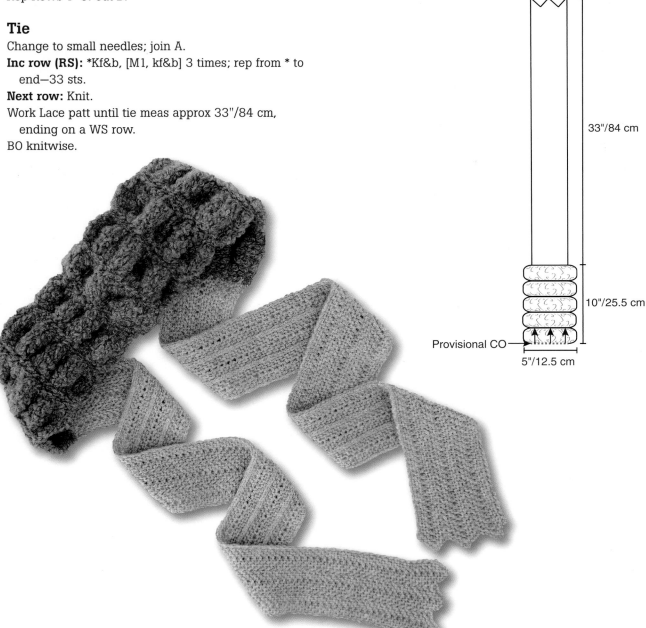

3¹/₂"/9 cm

33"/84 cm

10"/25.5 cm

Provisional CO →

5"/12.5 cm

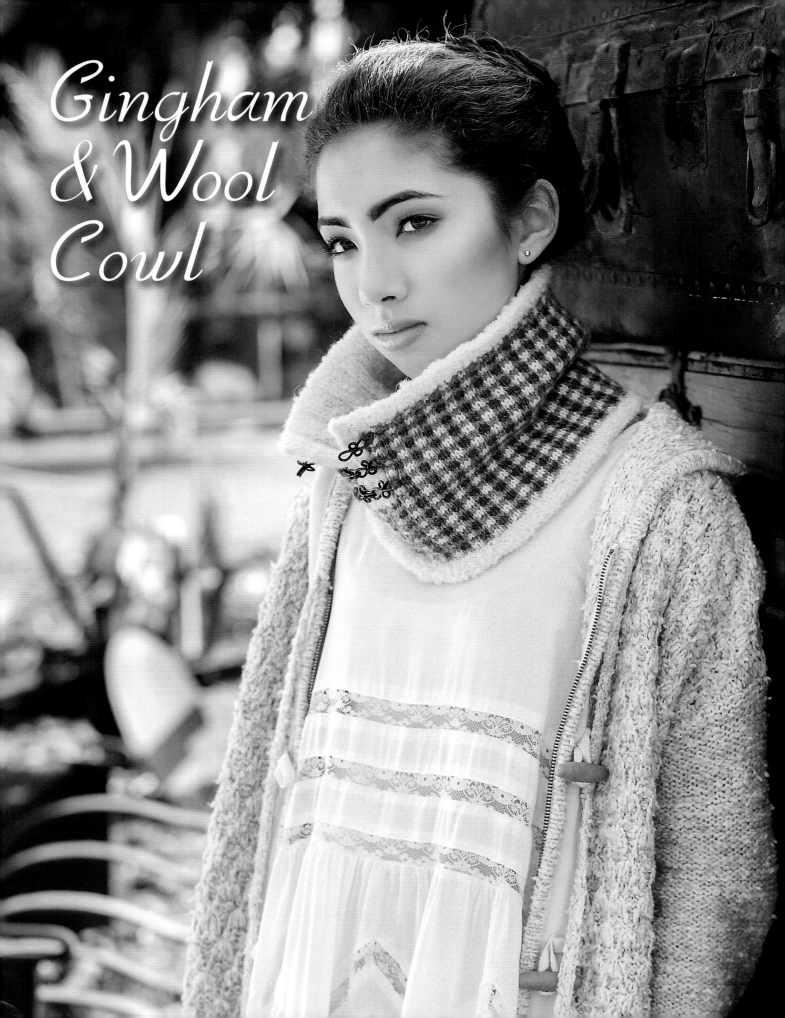

Gingham
& Wool
Cowl

FINISHED MEASUREMENTS

6½"/16.5 cm tall and 23"/58.5 cm circumference

YARN

Color A: 68 yds/62 m DK weight #3 yarn (shown in #782 Mid Brown, Rowan British Sheep Breeds DK Undyed; 100% British wool; 131 yds/120 m per 50 g skein)

Color B: 47 yds/43 m DK weight #3 yarn (shown in #780 Ecru, Rowan British Sheep Breeds DK Undyed; 100% British wool; 131 yds/120 m per 50 g skein)

Color C: 32 yds/29 m DK weight #3 yarn (shown in #781 Brown, Rowan British Sheep Breeds DK Undyed; 100% British wool; 131 yds/120 m per 50 g skein)

Color D: 173 yds/58 m bulky weight #5 yarn (shown in #316 Ecru Masham, Rowan British Sheep Breeds Fine Bouclé; 91% British wool, 9% nylon; 109 yds/100 m per 50 g skein)

NEDLES

- US 4/3.5 mm 24"/60 cm circular needle
- Set of US 4/3.5 mm double-pointed needles
- US 6/4 mm 24"/60 cm circular needle

Adjust needle sizes if necessary to obtain correct gauge.

NOTIONS

- Locking stitch markers in 2 colors (A and B)
- Stitch holders
- Tapestry needle
- 3 sets of decorative hooks and eyes

GAUGE

Using larger needle and A, B, or C, 24 sts and 56 rnds/rows in Check patt, blocked = 4"/10 cm square
Using larger needle and D, 16 sts and 26 rows in 2x2 Rib, blocked = 4"/10 cm square

PATTERN NOTES

- Project is worked in one piece, with bottom half of the lining worked first, followed by the bottom half of the outer "public" section, both of which are worked in the round. The top half is split for a placket opening, with both the public and lining sections worked flat. After the piece is complete, the edges of the lining are sewn together. Finally, a two-sided placket is worked.
- Carry non-working yarns up at beginning of the round by twisting the two yarns together.
- When slipping stitches, slip with working yarn held on WS.
- See page 134 for a photo tutorial on 3-needle BO.

PATTERN STITCHES

2x2 Rib, worked in rounds (multiple of 4 sts)
Patt rnd: *K2, p2; rep from * around.

2/2 Rib, worked in rows (multiple of 4 sts)
Row 1 (RS): K3, *p2, k2; rep from * to last st, k1.
Row 2 (WS): P3, *k2, p2; rep from * to last st, p1.
Rep Rows 1–2 for patt.

Cowl

Bottom Half of Lining

Using larger needle and D, CO 96 sts. Place marker A in third st and marker B in third st before end. Mark beg of rnd with another st marker and join, taking care not to twist sts.

Work in 2x2 Rib until piece meas 3½"/9 cm.

Folding rnd: Change to smaller circular needle; purl.

Public Side

Work 1 rnd in 2x2 Rib patt.

Change to larger needle; work 3 rnds in 2x2 Rib patt.

Inc rnd: With B, M1, *[k2, M1] 7 times, k2; rep from * to end, M1—140 sts. *Mark this rnd.*

Work 6-rnd Check patt until piece meas approx 3"/7.5 cm from marked Inc rnd, ending on Rnd 1.

Division rnd: With A, k2 and place these 2 sts on st holder; with B, k1, sl 1, *k2, sl 2; rep from * to last 8 sts, k2, sl 1, k1; place last 4 unworked sts on same holder with first 2 sts. Cut C—134 sts, with 6 center sts on holder.

Note: Piece will now be worked flat.

Beg with Row 6 (WS), work 6-row Check patt until piece meas approx 5½"/14 cm from marked Inc rnd, ending on Row 1.

Do not turn. Slide sts to other end of needle to work next row as RS row.

Dec row (RS): With B, *[k1, k2tog] 14 times, k2; rep from * to last 2 sts, k2—92 sts. *Mark this row.* Cut B.

Rejoin D; purl 1 row.

Work Rows 1–2 of 2/2 Rib patt (different from 2x2 Rib—see Pattern Stitches).

Change to smaller circular needle and work Row 1 of 2/2 Rib patt.

Folding row (WS): Knit.

Top Half of Lining

Work Row 1 of 2/2 Rib patt.

Change to larger circular needle; cont in 2/2 Rib patt until piece meas approx 3½"/9 cm from marked Dec row, ending on a WS row.

BO all sts.

Turn piece inside out; fold top and bottom halves of lining in at Folding rnds.

Sew CO edge to BO edge, lining up ends of BO edge between marker A and marker B.

Turn piece right side out.

**Check Pattern, worked in rounds
(multiple of 4 sts)**

Rnd 1: With A, knit.

Rnds 2–3: With B, *k2, sl 2; rep from * to end.

Rnd 4: With A, knit.

Rnds 5–6: With C, *sl 2, k2; rep from * to end.

Rep Rnds 1–6 for patt.

**Check Pattern, worked in rows
(multiple of 4 sts + 2)**

Row 1 (RS): With A, knit.

Row 2 (WS): With C, *p2, sl 2; rep from * to last 2 sts, p2.

Row 3: With C, k2, *sl 2, k2; rep from * to end.

Row 4: With A, purl.

Row 5: With B, k1, sl 1, *k2, sl 2; rep from * to last 4 sts, k2, sl 1, k1.

Row 6: With B, p1, sl 1, p2, *sl 2, p2; rep from * to last 2 sts, sl 1, p1.

Rep Rows 1–6 for patt.

Right Placket

With Color D and a dpn, with Public Side facing, starting at the base of the placket opening, pick up and knit 21 sts on Public Side (18 sts along Check patt section and 3 sts in bouclé section); with a second dpn, pick up and knit 21 sts along placket opening on Lining Side—42 sts.

Row 1 (WS): *(Lining Side):* P1, [k2, p2] 5 times; *(Public Side):* [p2, k2] 5 times, purl last st tog with closest st on holder at base of placket opening.

Row 2 (RS): *(Public Side):* Knit first st tog with closest st on holder, [p2, k2] 5 times; *(Lining Side):* [k2, p2] 5 times, k1.

Row 3: Rep Row 1.

With Public Side facing and using larger needle, join the two sides using 3-needle BO.

Left Placket

Turn piece inside out.

With Color D and a dpn, with Lining Side facing, starting at the base of the placket opening, pick up and knit 21 sts along placket opening on Lining Side; with a second dpn, pick up and knit 21 sts on Public Side of placket opening (3 sts in bouclé section and 18 sts along Check patt section)—42 sts.

Row 1 (WS): *(Public Side):* Purl first st tog with closest st on holder, [k2, p2] 5 times; *(Lining Side):* [p2, k2] 5 times, p1.

Row 2 (RS): *(Lining Side):* K1, [p2, k2] 5 times; *(Public Side):* [k2, p2] 5 times, knit last st tog with closest st on holder.

Row 3: Rep Row 1.

With Public Side facing, using larger needle, join the two sides using 3-needle BO.

Finishing

Weave in ends.

Sew selvedges of Right and Left Placket to BO edge on Lining Side.

Block to shape.

Using the tapestry needle, sew hooks and eyes where indicated on photo.

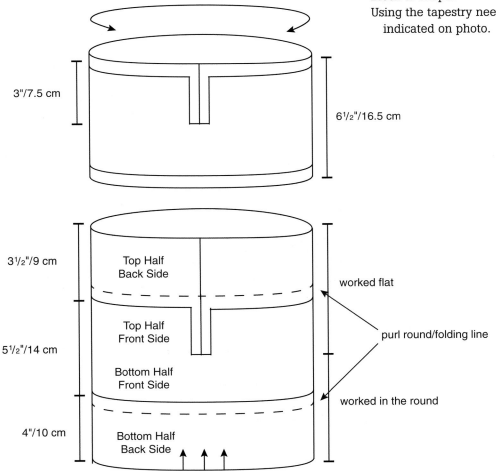

23"/58.5 cm

3"/7.5 cm

6½"/16.5 cm

3½"/9 cm

Top Half
Back Side

worked flat

Top Half
Front Side

purl round/folding line

5½"/14 cm

Bottom Half
Front Side

worked in the round

4"/10 cm

Bottom Half
Back Side

Kerchief Cowls, Western Style

Both of these cowls are reminiscent of a cowboy's bandana—with the triangular tip in front. They add a Western flair to any outfit, and also provide an extra layer of warmth under a coat.

Sunset Kerchief

Though the Sunset Kerchief is worn in a manner similar to the Cowboy Cowl, it has a distinctly different shape, more akin to a triangular shawl. Worked from the bottom up, the pattern uses multiple colors to achieve an ombré effect with splashes of brightly colored gold stripes running through it. The stitch pattern is primarily stockinette stitch, with sporadic stripes of reverse stockinette stitch. The knitter will need to pay attention to color changes and increases along the edges.

Cowboy Cowl

The Cowboy Cowl is slightly more complex due to the patterning and shaping. It is knit from the top down using a variety of textures, including a simple lace pattern that runs down the center of the kerchief. The top edge is turned under so that it stands upright, followed by a draped cowl section on top that can be adjusted to a wider, longer silhouette by leaving the lower buttons undone. The most challenging aspect of the cowl is the shaping toward the bottom of the kerchief. A chart is provided as well as row-by-row instructions to navigate through the decreases of the lace patterning.

Sunset
Kerchief

FINISHED MEASUREMENTS

8"/20.5 cm wide and 57"/145 cm long

YARN

Color A: 36 yds/33 m DK weight #3 yarn (shown in Smokestack, Madelinetosh Tosh DK; 100% superwash merino wool; 225 yds/206 m per 100 g skein)

Color B: 108 yds/99 m DK weight #3 yarn (shown in Silver Fox, Madelinetosh Tosh DK; 100% superwash merino wool; 225 yds/206 m per 100 g skein)

Color C: 157 yds/144 m DK weight #3 yarn (shown in Antler, Madelinetosh Tosh DK; 100% superwash merino wool; 225 yds/206 m per 100 g skein)

Color D: 248 yds/227 m DK weight #3 yarn (shown in Candlewick, Madelinetosh Tosh DK; 100% superwash merino wool; 225 yds/206 m per 100 g skein)

NEEDLES

- Set of US 6/4 mm straight knitting needles

Adjust needle size if necessary to obtain correct gauge.

NOTIONS

- Locking stitch marker
- Tapestry needle

GAUGE

22 sts and 33 rows in St st = 4"/10 cm square, blocked.

PATTERN NOTES

- The cowl is knit in one piece from the bottom up.
- Slip stitches with yarn in back on RS rows and yarn in front on WS rows.
- Carry non-working yarn up the side by twisting the two yarns together.
- See page 135 for a photo tutorial on short-row shaping.

SPECIAL STITCHES

Central double decrease (cdd): Sl 2 sts as if to knit 2 together, knit 1, pass slipped sts over—2 sts dec'd.

Make 1 Left (M1L): Insert LH needle, from front to back, under strand of yarn that runs between next st on LH needle and last st on RH needle; knit this st through back loop—left-slanting inc, 1 st inc'd.

Make 1 Right (M1R): Insert LH needle, from back to front, under strand of yarn which runs between next st on LH needle and last st on RH needle; knit this st through front loop—right-slanting inc, 1 st inc'd.

PATTERN STITCH

Seed Stitch

Row 1: *K1, p1; rep from * to end.
Row 2: Knit the purl sts and purl the knit sts.
Rep Row 2 for patt.

Cowl

Body

With A, CO 2 sts.

Set-up row (WS): Knit.

Row 1 (RS): K1, M1R, k1—3 sts.

Row 2: Knit.

Row 3: K1, M1R, k1, M1L, k1—5 sts.

Row 4: K2, p1, k2.

Row 5: K2, M1R, knit to last 2 sts, M1L, k2—2 sts inc'd.

Row 6: K2, purl to last 2 sts, k2.

Rows 7–30: Rep Rows 5–6—31 sts after working Row 30. Do not cut A.

Row 31: Join D; *sl 2, k2; rep from * to last 3 sts, w&t. (3 sts rem unworked.)

Row 32: *K2, sl 2; rep from * to end. Cut D.

Rows 33–58: With A, rep Rows 5–6, hiding wrapped st on Row 33 when you come to it—57 sts. Cut A.

Rows 59–84: Join B; rep Rows 5–6—83 sts. Do not cut B.

Rows 85–86: Join D; rep Rows 31–32. Cut D.

Rows 87–112: With B, rep Rows 5–6, hiding wrapped st on Row 87 when you come to it—109 sts. Cut B.

Rows 113–138: Join C; rep Rows 5–6—135 sts. Do not cut C.

Rows 139–140: Join D, rep Rows 31–32. Cut D.

Rows 141–166: With C, rep Rows 5–6, hiding wrapped st on Row 141 when you come to it—161 sts. Cut C.

Row 167: Join D; k2, M1R, knit to last 2 sts, M1L, k2—163 sts.

Rows 168 & 170: K2, work Seed st to last 2 sts, k2.

Rows 169 & 171: K2, M1R, work Seed st to last 2 sts, M1L, k2—165 sts.

Row 172: Rep Row 168.

Center Band and Ties

Place marker after first 67 sts.

Division row (RS): K2, M1R, work Seed st to marker, remove marker, BO next 32 sts, k2tog *(note: the last bound-off st is passed over the k2tog)*, work Seed st to last 2 sts, M1L, k2—68 sts rem for each side.

Left Tie

Worked over 68 sts.

Row 1 (WS): K2, work Seed st to last 6 sts, [k2tog] twice, k2—2 sts dec'd.

Row 2 (RS): K4, work Seed st to last 2 sts, M1L, k2—1 st inc'd.

Rows 3–96: [Rep Rows 1–2] 47 times—20 sts.

Row 97: K2, work Seed st to last 4 sts, k2tog, k2—1 st dec'd.

Row 98: Rep Row 2—1 st inc'd.

Row 99: Rep Row 1—2 sts dec'd.

Row 100: Rep Row 2—1 st inc'd.

Rows 101–148: [Rep Rows 97–100] 12 times—7 sts.

Row 149: K1, [k2tog] twice, k2—5 sts.

Row 150: K2, p1, M1L, k2—6 sts.

Row 151: K2, k2tog, k2—5 sts.

Row 152: K3, M1L, k2—6 sts.

Row 153: K1, cdd, k2—4 sts.

Row 154: K2, M1L, k2—5 sts.

Row 155: K1, k2tog, k2—4 sts.

Row 156: K2, M1L, k2—5 sts.

Row 157: K1, cdd, k1—3 sts.

Row 158: K1, M1L, k2—4 sts.

Row 159: K1, k2tog, k1—3 sts.

Row 160: K1, M1L, k2—4 sts.

Row 161: Cdd, k1—2 sts.

Row 162: K1, M1L, k1—3 sts.

Row 163: K1, k2tog—2 sts.

Row 164: K1, M1L, k1—3 sts.

Row 165: Cdd.

Pull yarn through last st.

Right Tie

Worked over 68 sts.

Row 1 (WS): Join D; k2, [ssk] twice, work Seed st to last 2 sts, k2—2 sts dec'd.

Row 2 (RS): K2, M1R, work Seed st to last 4 sts, k4—1 st inc'd.

Rows 3–96: [Rep Rows 1–2] 47 times—20 sts.

Row 97: K2, ssk, k1, work Seed st to last 2 sts, k2—1 st dec'd.

Row 98: Rep Row 2—1 st inc'd.

Row 99: Rep Row 1—2 sts dec'd.

Row 100: Rep Row 2—1 st inc'd.

Rows 101–148: [Rep Rows 97–100] 12 times—7 sts.

Row 149: K2, [ssk] twice, k1—5 sts.

Row 150: K2, M1R, p1, k2—6 sts.

Row 151: K2, ssk, k2—5 sts.

Row 152: K2, M1R, k3—6 sts.

Row 153: K2, cdd, k1—4 sts.

Row 154: K2, M1R, k2—5 sts.

Row 155: K2, ssk, k1—4 sts.

Row 156: K2, M1R, k2—5 sts.

Row 157: K1, cdd, k1—3 sts.

Row 158: K2, M1R, k1—4 sts.

Row 159: K1, ssk, k1—3 sts.

Row 160: K2, M1R, k1—4 sts.

Row 161: K1, cdd—2 sts.

Row 162: K1, M1R, k1—3 sts.

Row 163: Ssk, k1—2 sts.

Row 164: K1, M1R, k1—3 sts.

Row 165: Cdd.

Pull yarn through last st.

Finishing

Block flat. Weave in ends.

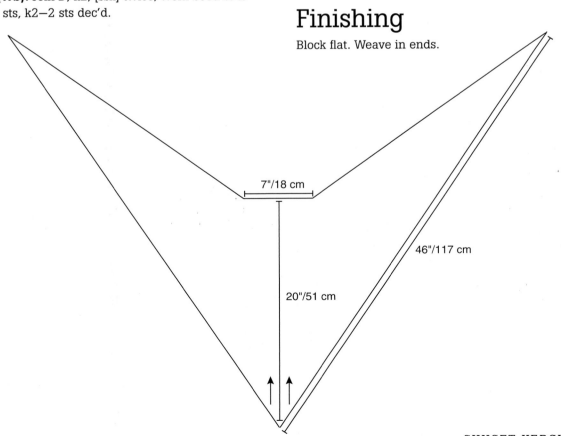

7"/18 cm

20"/51 cm

46"/117 cm

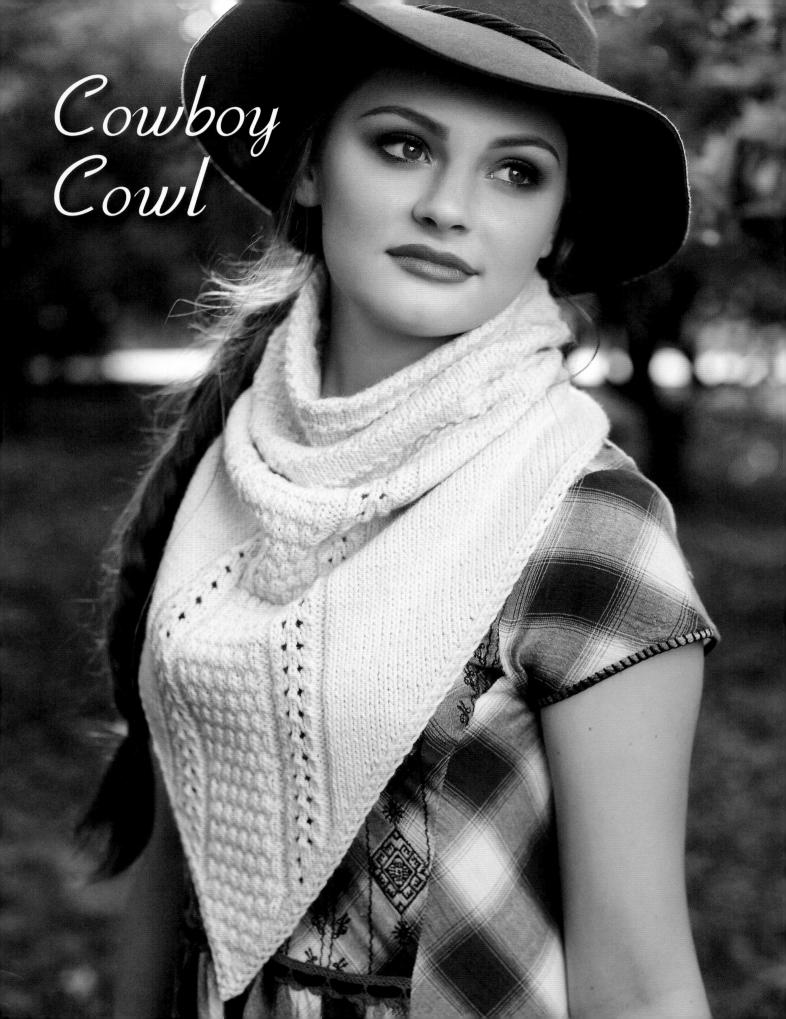

Cowboy Cowl

FINISHED MEASUREMENTS

24"/61 cm wide (at widest point) and 25"/63.5 long

YARN

387 yds/354 m worsted weight #4 yarn (shown in Ivory, Shibui Knits Merino Alpaca; 50% baby alpaca, 50% merino wool; 131 yds/120 m per 100 g)

NEEDLES

✤ Set of US 8/5 mm straight knitting needles
✤ US G-6/4 mm crochet hook (for button loops)
Adjust needle size if necessary to obtain correct gauge.

NOTIONS

✤ Five ½"/1.25 cm buttons
✤ Tapestry needle

GAUGE

20 sts and 28 rows in St st = 4"/10 cm square, blocked

PATTERN NOTES

✤ Cowl is knit flat from the top down.
✤ Slip first stitch of every row (except first and last rows) purlwise with yarn in front.
✤ Top edge of cowl is folded down and stitched in place.

SPECIAL STITCHES

Sk2p: Sl 1 st as if to knit, knit 2 sts tog, pass slipped st over—left-slanting dec, 2 sts dec'd.

Make 1 Left (M1L): Insert LH needle, from front to back, under strand of yarn that runs between next st on LH needle and last st on RH needle; knit this st through back loop—left-slanting inc, 1 st inc'd.

Make 1 Right (M1R): Insert LH needle, from back to front, under strand of yarn which runs between next st on LH needle and last st on RH needle; knit this st through front loop—right-slanting inc, 1 st inc'd.

Cowl

CO 102 sts.

Row 1 (WS): K2, *p2, k2; rep from * to end.

Row 2 (RS): Sl 1 wyif, k1, *k2, p2; rep from * to last 4 sts, k4.

Row 3: Sl 1, k1, *p2, k2; rep from * to end.

Rows 4–7: Rep Rows 2–3 twice.

Rows 8 & 10: Sl 1, knit to end.

Rows 9, 11, & 13: Sl 1, k1, purl to last 2 sts, k2.

Row 12 (Inc row): Sl 1, k1, M1R, knit to last 2 sts, M1L, k2—2 sts inc'd.

Row 14: Sl 1, k1, *k1, p1; rep from * to last 2 sts, k2; pm in first and last sts for first rep (Row 14) only (markers are for turning row).

Row 15: Sl 1, k1, *p1, k1; rep from * to last 2 sts, k2.
The last 6 rows establish patt with 2-st slipped garter selvedge on both edges.

Rows 16–69: Rep [Rows 10–15] 9 more times—122 sts.

Row 70: Sl 1, knit to end.

Row 71: Sl 1, k1, p44, pm, p30, pm, purl to last 2 sts, k2.

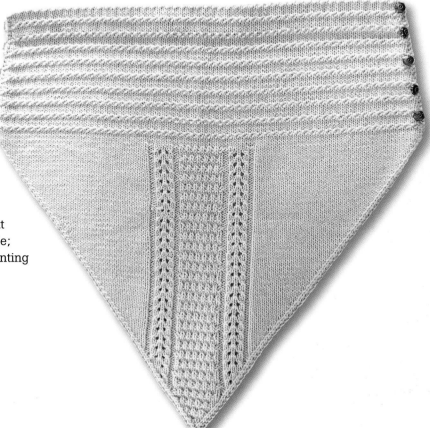

Kerchief

Row 1 (RS): Sl 1, k1, ssk, knit to marker, sl m, p2, k5, p2, [k1, p1] 6 times, p2, k5, p2, sl m, knit to last 4 sts, k2tog, k2—2 sts dec'd.

Row 2 (WS): Sl 1, k1, purl to marker, k2, p5, k2, [k1, p1] 6 times, k2, p5, k2, purl to last 2 sts, k2.

Row 3: Sl 1, k1, ssk, knit to marker, p2, k2tog, yo, k1, yo, skp, p2, k12, p2, k2tog, yo, k1, yo, ssk, p2, knit to last 4 sts, k2tog, k2—2 sts dec'd.

Row 4: Sl 1, k1, purl to marker, k2, p5, k2, p12, k2, p5, k2, purl to last 2 sts, k2.

Row 5: Sl 1, k1, ssk, knit to marker, p2, k5, p2, [p1, k1] 6 times, p2, k5, p2, knit to last 4 sts, k2tog, k2—2 sts dec'd.

Row 6: Sl 1, k1, purl to marker, k2, p5, k2, [p1, k1] 6 times, k2, p5, k2, purl to last 2 sts, k2.

Rows 7–8: Rep Rows 3–4.

Rows 9–80: Rep [Rows 1–8] 9 times—42 sts.

Rows 81–84: Rep Rows 1–4—38 sts.

If desired, refer to chart for Rows 85–121.

Row 85 (RS): Sl 1, k1, ssk, p2, k5, p2, [p1, k1] 6 times, p2, k5, p2, k2tog, k2—36 sts.

Row 86 (and all WS rows): Maintaining established 2-st slipped garter selvedge, work all other sts as they present themselves, i.e. knit the knit sts and purl the purl sts and yo's.

Row 87: Sl 1, k1, ssk, p1, k2tog, yo, k1, yo, ssk, p2, k12, p2, k2tog, yo, k1, yo, ssk, p1, k2tog, k2—34 sts.

Row 89: Sl 1, k1, ssk, k5, p2, [k1, p1] 6 times, p2, k5, k2tog, k2—32 sts.

Row 91: Sl 1, k1, ssk, k2, yo, ssk, p2, k12, p2, k2tog, yo, k2, k2tog, k2—30 sts.

Row 93: Sl 1, k1, ssk, k3, p2, [p1, k1] 6 times, p2, k3, k2tog, k2—28 sts.

Row 95: Sl 1, k1, ssk, yo, ssk, p2, k12, p2, k2tog, yo, k2tog, k2—26 sts.

Row 97: Sl 1, k1, ssk, k1, p2, [k1, p1] 6 times, p2, k1, k2tog, k2—24 sts.

Row 99: Sl 1, k1, ssk, p2, k12, p2, k2tog, k2—22 sts.

Row 101: Sl 1, k1, ssk, p1, [p1, k1] 6 times, p1, k2tog, k2—20 sts.

Row 103: Sl 1, k1, ssk, k12, k2tog, k2—18 sts.

Row 105: Sl 1, k1, ssk, [p1, k1] 5 times, k2tog, k2—16 sts.

Row 107: Sl 1, k1, ssk, k8, k2tog, k2—14 sts.

Row 109: Sl 1, k1, ssk, [k1, p1] 3 times, k2tog, k2—12 sts.

Row 111: Sl 1, k1, ssk, k4, k2tog, k2—10 sts.

Row 113: Sl 1, k1, ssk, p1, k1, k2tog, k2—8 sts.

Row 115: Sl 1, k1, ssk, k2tog, k2—6 sts.

Row 117: Sl 1, k1, ssk, k2—5 sts.

Row 119: Sl 1, sk2p, k1—3 sts.

Row 120: Sl 1, k2.
Row 121: Sk2p—1 st.
Pull yarn through last st.

Finishing

Weave in all ends and block lightly.

Turn top edge under at marked row (see "fold line" on schematic below) and stitch in place on WS using whipstitch.

Crochet 5 button loops along side edge of Cowl section as follows: Mark 5 button-loop positions along the side edge as indicated on the schematic.

Row 1 (WS): With WS facing, starting at top of button-hole edge, insert crochet hook between the selvedge st and first st; working from right to left, crochet a row of slip sts to the end of the button-loop edge. Turn.

Row 2 (RS): *Crochet a chain large enough for the button to slip through; insert hook between crochet slip st and selvedge st and work a slip st to attach button-loop chain; work slip st to next marked button-loop position; rep from * to end of button-loop edge, ending by joining last button-loop chain to edge with slip st.

Sew on 5 buttons along the opposite edge of Cowl section.

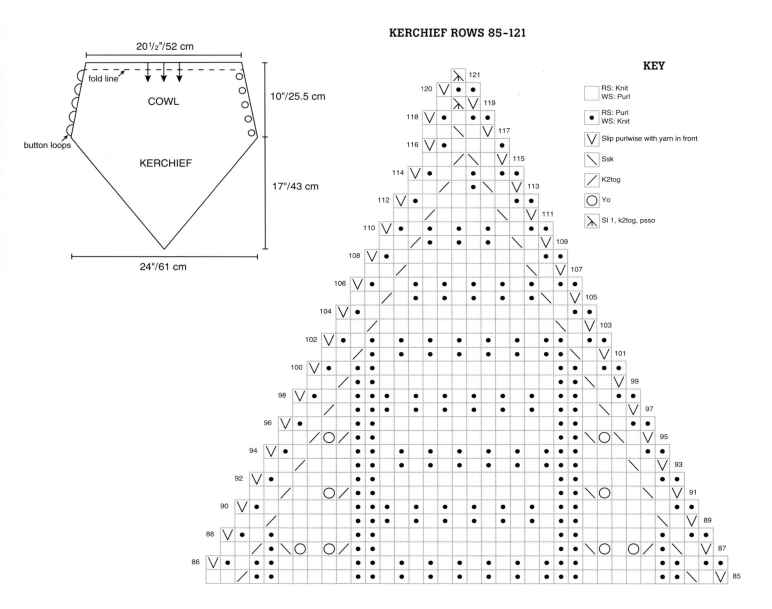

KERCHIEF ROWS 85–121

KEY

	RS: Knit / WS: Purl
•	RS: Purl / WS: Knit
V	Slip purlwise with yarn in front
╲	Ssk
╱	K2tog
O	Yo
⅄	Sl 1, k2tog, psso

Ballet Beauties

These two ascots are delicate and feminine, despite the fact that they are worked up in bulky yarns. They display an avant-garde approach to knitted scarves and are worn as true statement pieces.

Primrose Ascot

The Primrose Ascot has a Bohemian feel that works as well with a strappy dress and cardigan on a cool summer night as it does with a tapestry coat in the middle of winter. This scarf is a very simple, quick knit, even with its lovely details. The asymmetrical leaves are created by picking up and knitting stitches from the body of the ascot and require only basic shaping techniques. The rose is made separately and sewn on.

Bow Tie Ascot

The Bow Tie Ascot includes more complex shaping and cables, but is still a relatively quick knit. The shape is similar to that of a man's bow tie and is sewn to form a pull-through slit for the end. Reversible cables make a decorative non-rolling scalloped edge.

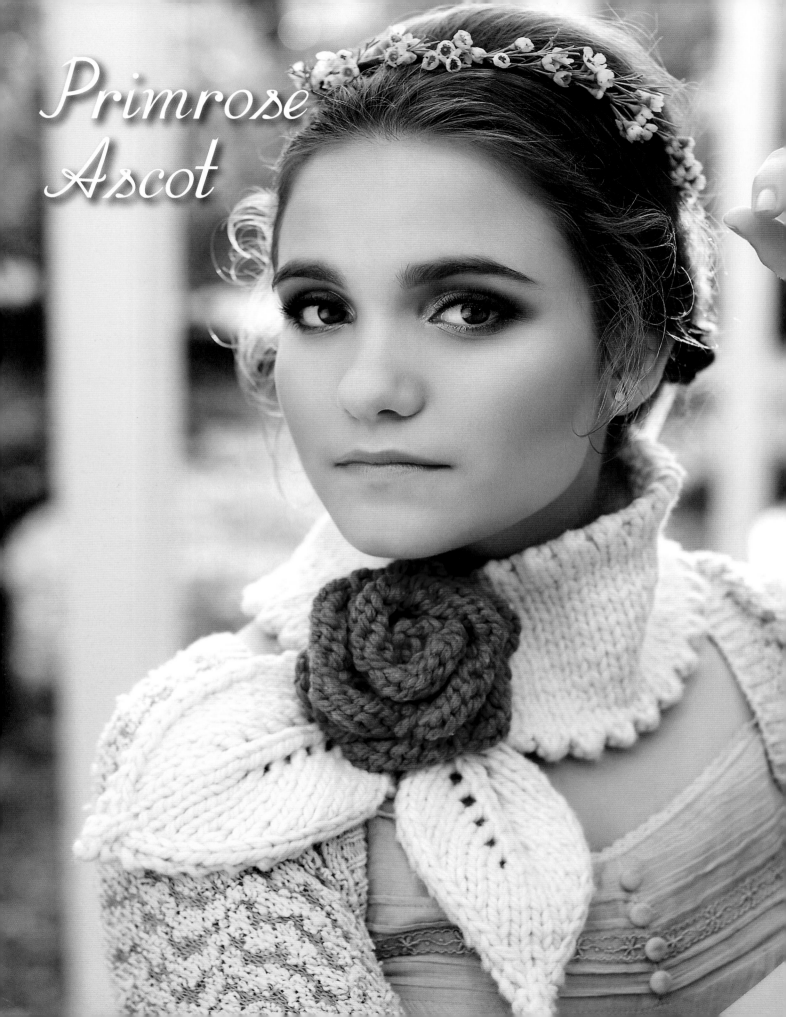

Primrose
Ascot

FINISHED MEASUREMENTS

4½"/11.5 cm wide and 34"/86.5 cm long

YARN

Color A: 91 yds/83.5 m chunky weight #5 yarn (shown in #7200 Soapstone, Spud & Chloë Outer; 65% superwash wool, 35% organic cotton; 60 yds/55 m per 100 g skein)

Color B: 20 yds/18.5 m chunky weight #5 yarn (shown in #7205 Sequoia, Spud & Chloë Outer; 65% superwash wool, 35% organic cotton; 60 yds/55 m per 100 g skein)

NEEDLES

❀ US 8/5 mm 24"/60 cm or longer circular needle
❀ 2 US 11/8 mm 24"/60 cm or longer circular needles
Adjust both needle sizes (up or down) if necessary to obtain correct gauge.

NOTIONS

❀ Stitch holder
❀ Locking stitch markers
❀ Tapestry needle

GAUGE

Using larger needle, 13 sts and 16 rows in St st = 4"/10 cm square, blocked

PATTERN NOTES

❀ Body of scarf is worked horizontally with A. Stitches are picked up along one short side to work a ribbed slit, followed by a large leaf. Stitches are picked up along other short side to work a single layer of rib, followed by a small leaf.
❀ Rose is worked separately with B, then sewn on.
❀ See page 133 for a photo tutorial on 3-needle join.

SPECIAL STITCHES

Central double decrease (cdd): Sl 2 sts as if to knit 2 tog, knit 1, pass slipped sts over—2 sts dec'd.

Scarf

Body

Using larger needle and A, CO 59 sts. Do not join.

Row 1 (RS): Knit.

Row 2 (WS): Purl.

Row 3 (Eyelet row): *K2tog, yo; rep from * to last st, k1.

Rows 4–20: Work in St st.

Row 21: Rep Row 3.

Row 22: Purl.

Row 23: Knit.

BO all sts.

Fold both edges toward WS at Eyelet rows to form picot edges; tack or sew loosely in place to maintain elasticity.

Slit Side

With RS facing, using smaller needle and A, pick up and knit 18 sts along one short side of Body.

Divide sts for slit: With RS facing and 2 larger needles held parallel, *sl 1 to front needle, sl 1 to back needle; rep from * to last st, sl 1 to front needle—9 sts on front needle, 9 sts on back needle.

Slit Front

Row 1 (WS): P1, *k1, p1; rep from * to end.
Row 2 (RS): K1, *p1, k1; rep from * to end.
Rows 3–8: Rep Rows 1–2.
Row 9: Rep Row 1. Do not cut yarn.

Slit Back

Join A and work the same as Slit Front. Cut yarn.

Close Slit

With RS facing and using larger needle, join Slit Front to Slit Back using 3-needle join—9 sts.

Large Leaf

Row 1 (WS): Ssk, purl to last 2 sts, k2tog—7 sts.
Row 2 (RS): K3, yo, k1, yo, k3—9 sts.
Row 3 and all WS rows: K1, purl to last st, k1.
Row 4: K4, yo, k1, yo, k4—11 sts.
Row 6: K5, yo, k1, yo, k5—13 sts.
Row 8: K6, yo, k1, yo, k6—15 sts.
Rows 10 & 12: K1, ssk, k4, yo, k1, yo, k4, k2tog, k1.
Row 14: K1, ssk, k9, k2tog, k1—13 sts.
Row 16: K1, ssk, k7, k2tog, k1—11 sts.
Row 18: K1, ssk, k5, k2tog, k1—9 sts.
Row 20: K1, ssk, k3, k2tog, k1—7 sts.
Row 22: K1, ssk, k1, k2tog, k1—5 sts.
Row 24: K1, cdd, k1—3 sts.
Row 26: Cdd.
Pull yarn through last st and cut.

Pull-Through Side

With RS facing, using smaller needle and A, pick up and knit 7 sts along rem short end of Body.
Row 1 (WS): P1, *k1, p1; rep from * to end.
Row 2 (RS): K1, *p1, k1; rep from * to end.
Rows 3–10: Rep Rows 1–2.

Small Leaf

Change to larger needle.
Row 1 (WS): Ssk, purl to last 2 sts, k2tog—5 sts.
Row 2 (RS): K2, yo, k1, yo, k2—7 sts.
Row 3 and all WS rows: K1, purl to last st, k1.
Row 4: K3, yo, k1, yo, k3—9 sts.
Row 6: K4, yo, k1, yo, k4—11 sts.
Row 8: K5, yo, k1, yo, k5—13 sts.
Rows 10 & 12: K1, ssk, k3, yo, k1, yo, k3, k2tog, k1.
Row 14: K1, ssk, k7, k2tog, k1—11 sts.
Row 16: K1, ssk, k5, k2tog, k1—9 sts.
Row 18: K1, ssk, k3, k2tog, k1—7 sts.
Row 20: K1, ssk, k1, k2tog, k1—5 sts.
Row 22: K1, cdd, k1—3 sts.
Row 24: Cdd.

Pull yarn through last st and cut.

Rose

Using larger needle and B, CO 60 sts.
Rows 1 (WS)–3: Work in St st.
Row 4 (RS): *K5, then rotate LH needle counterclockwise 360 degrees to twist the fabric; rep from * to end.
Row 5: Purl.
Row 6: K2tog to end—30 sts.
Row 7: P2tog to end—15 sts.
Row 8: K1, k2tog to end—8 sts.
Cut yarn, leaving a 36"/91.5 cm tail.
Use tapestry needle to run tail through rem sts, pull tightly, and secure.
Twist rose into a spiral, using tail to secure in place. Do not cut tail.

Finishing

Block Body and Leaves to shape.
Use tail to sew Rose to Slit Front.

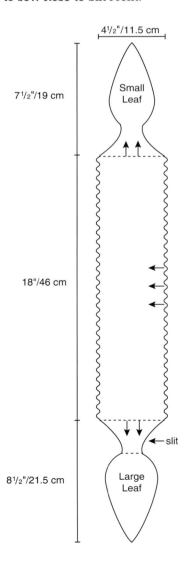

Bow Tie Ascot

FINISHED MEASUREMENTS

6½"/16.5 cm wide and 30"/76 cm long (with bow constructed)

YARN

260 yds/238 m worsted weight #4 yarn (shown in #2008 Light Pink, Blue Sky Alpacas Worsted Hand Dyes; 50% royal alpaca, 50% merino wool; 100 yds/91 m per 100 g skein)

NEEDLES

❦ Set of US 8/5 mm straight knitting needles

Adjust needle size if necessary to obtain correct gauge.

NOTIONS

❦ Stitch markers
❦ Cable needle
❦ Tapestry needle

GAUGE

18 sts and 36 rows in Garter st = 4"/10 cm square, blocked

PATTERN NOTES

❦ Scarf is knit in one piece, end to end.
❦ Because of the way the bow is constructed, the RS and WS are switched between the Bow and the Body, at which point the RS becomes the WS and the WS becomes the RS. The last row of the Second Half of Bow is a RS row and the next row (first row of the Body) is also a RS row.
❦ See page 135 for a photo tutorial on short-row shaping.

SPECIAL STITCHES/TECHNIQUES

5/5 LC-Purl Rib: Slip 5 sts to cn and hold in front; [p1, k1] twice, p1; [p1, k1] twice, p1 from cn.

5/5 RC-Purl Rib: Slip 5 sts to cn and hold in back; [p1, k1] twice, p1; [p1, k1] twice, p1 from cn.

Make 1 Left (M1L): Insert LH needle, from front to back, under strand of yarn that runs between next st on LH needle and last st on RH needle; knit this st through back loop—left-slanting inc, 1 st inc'd.

Make 1 Right (M1R): Insert LH needle, from back to front, under strand of yarn which runs between next st on LH needle and last st on RH needle; knit this st through front loop—right-slanting inc, 1 st inc'd

Scarf

First Half of Bow

CO 21 sts.

Row 1 (RS): [P1, k1] twice, p2, [k1, p1] twice, pm, k1, pm, [p1, k1] twice, p2, [k1, p1] twice.

Row 2 and all WS rows: [K1, p1] twice, k2, [p1, k1] twice, sl m, knit to next marker, sl m, [k1, p1] twice, k2, [p1, k1] twice.

Row 3: [P1, k1] twice, p2, [k1, p1] twice, sl m, k1, M1L, sl m, [p1, k1] twice, p2, [k1, p1] twice—22 sts.

Row 5: 5/5 LC-Purl Rib, sl m, M1R, k2, M1L, sl m, 5/5 RC-Purl Rib—24 sts.

Row 7: [P1, k1] twice, p2, [k1, p1] twice, sl m, M1R, k4, M1L, sl m, [p1, k1] twice, p2, [k1, p1] twice—26 sts.

Row 9: [P1, k1] twice, p2, [k1, p1] twice, sl m, M1R, k6, M1L, sl m, [p1, k1] twice, p2, [k1, p1] twice —28 sts.

Row 11: 5/5 LC-Purl Rib, sl m, M1R, k3, M1R, k2, M1L, k3, M1L, sl m, 5/5 RC-Purl Rib—32 sts.

Rows 13 & 15: [P1, k1] twice, p2, [k1, p1] twice, knit to next marker, [p1, k1] twice, p2, [k1, p1] twice.

Row 17: 5/5 LC-Purl Rib, knit to next marker, 5/5 RC-Purl Rib.

Row 18: Rep Row 2.

Rows 19–48: Rep [Rows 13–18] 5 more times.

Row 49: Rep Row 13.

Row 51: [P1, k1] twice, p2, [k1, p1] twice, sl m, [ssk] twice, k4, [k2tog] twice, sl m, [p1, k1] twice, p2, [k1, p1] twice—28 sts.

Row 53: 5/5 LC-Purl Rib, sl m, ssk, k4, k2tog, sl m, 5/5 RC-Purl Rib—26 sts.

Row 55: [P1, k1] twice, p2, [k1, p1] twice, sl m, ssk, k2, k2tog, sl m, [p1, k1] twice, p2, [k1, p1] twice—24 sts.

Row 57: [P1, k1] twice, p2, [k1, p1] twice, sl m, ssk, k2tog, sl m, [p1, k1] twice, p2, [k1, p1] twice—22 sts.

Row 59: 5/5 LC-Purl Rib, sl m, ssk, sl m, 5/5 RC-Purl Rib—21 sts.

Row 60: [K1, p1] twice, k2, [p1, k1] twice, p1, [k1, p1] twice, k2, [p1, k1] twice.

Second Half of Bow

Row 1 (RS): [P1, k1] twice, p2, [k1, p1] 5 times, p1, [k1, p1] twice.

Row 2: [K1, p1] twice, k2, [p1, k1] twice, p1, [k1, p1] twice, k2, [p1, k1] twice.

Row 3: [P1, k1] twice, p2, [k1, p1] twice, sl m, k1, M1L, sl m, [p1, k1] twice, p2, [k1, p1] twice—22 sts.

Row 4 and all WS rows: [K1, p1] twice, k2, [p1, k1] twice, sl m, knit to next marker, sl m, [k1, p1] twice, k2, [p1, k1] twice.

Row 5: 5/5 RC-Purl Rib, sl m, M1R, k2, M1L, sl m, 5/5 LC-Purl Rib—24 sts.

Row 7: [P1, k1] twice, p2, [k1, p1] twice, sl m, M1R, k4, M1L, sl m, [p1, k1] twice, p2, [k1, p1] twice—26 sts.

Row 9: [P1, k1] twice, p2, [k1, p1] twice, sl m, M1R, k6, M1L, sl m, [p1, k1] twice, p2, [k1, p1] twice—28 sts.

Row 11: 5/5 RC-Purl Rib, sl m, M1R, k3, M1R, k2, M1L, k3, M1L, sl m, 5/5 LC-Purl Rib—32 sts.

Rows 13 & 15: [P1, k1] twice, p2, [k1, p1] twice, knit to next marker, [p1, k1] twice, p2, [k1, p1] twice.

Row 17: 5/5 RC-Purl Rib, knit to next marker, 5/5 LC-Purl Rib.

Row 18: Rep Row 4.

Rows 19–48: Rep [Rows 13–18] 5 more times.

Row 49: Rep Row 13.

Row 51: [P1, k1] twice, p2, [k1, p1] twice, sl m, [ssk] twice, k4, [k2tog] twice, sl m, [p1, k1] twice, p2, [k1, p1] twice—28 sts.

Row 53: 5/5 RC-Purl Rib, sl m, ssk, k4, k2tog, sl m, 5/5 LC-Purl Rib—26 sts.

Row 55: [P1, k1] twice, p2, [k1, p1] twice, sl m, ssk, k2, k2tog, sl m, [p1, k1] twice, p2, [k1, p1] twice—24 sts.

Row 57: [P1, k1] twice, p2, [k1, p1] twice, sl m, ssk, k2tog, sl m, [p1, k1] twice, p2, [k1, p1] twice—22 sts.

Row 59: 5/5 RC-Purl Rib, ssk, 5/5 LC-Purl Rib—21 sts.

Rows 60 & 62: [K1, p1] twice, k2, [p1, k1] twice, p1, [k1, p1] twice, k2, [p1, k1] twice.

Rows 61 & 63: Rep Row 1.

Body

Note: WS and RS are switched here, so next row is a RS row.

Row 1 (RS): 5/5 LC-Purl Rib, sl m, M1R, k1, M1L, sl m, 5/5 RC-Purl Rib—23 sts.

Row 2 and all WS rows: [K1, p1] twice, k2, [p1, k1] twice, sl m, knit to next marker, sl m, [k1, p1] twice, k2, [p1, k1] twice.

Row 3: [P1, k1] twice, p2, [k1, p1] twice, sl m, [M1R, k1] twice, M1L, k1, M1L, sl m, [p1, k1] twice, p2, [k1, p1] twice—27 sts.

Row 5: [P1, k1] twice, p2, [k1, p1] twice, sl m, [M1R, k1] twice, k1, M1R, k1, M1L, k1, [k1, M1L] twice, sl m, [p1, k1] twice, p2, [k1, p1] twice—33 sts.

Row 7: 5/5 LC-Purl Rib, sl m, [M1R, k2] 3 times, k1, [k2, M1L] 3 times, sl m, 5/5 RC-Purl Rib—39 sts.

Row 9: [P1, k1] twice, p2, [k1, p1] twice, sl m, M1R, knit to next marker, M1L, sl m, [p1, k1] twice, p2, [k1, p1] twice—41 sts.

Row 11: [P1, k1] twice, p2, [k1, p1] twice, knit to next marker, [p1, k1] twice, p2, [k1, p1] twice.

Row 13: 5/5 LC-Purl Rib, knit to next marker, 5/5 RC-Purl Rib.

Row 14: Rep Row 2.

Rows 15 & 17: Rep Row 11.

Row 19: Rep Row 13.

Rows 20–25: Rep Rows 14–19.

Rows 26–31:

Short Row Set 1: *(WS)* [K1, p1] twice, k2, [p1, k1] twice, k7, w&t; *(RS)* work in patt to end.

Short Row Set 2: Hiding wrap when you come to it, [k1, p1] twice, k2, [p1, k1] twice, k14, w&t; work in patt to end.

Short Row Set 3: [K1, p1] twice, k2, [p1, k1] twice, k20, w&t; knit to marker, 5/5 RC-Purl Rib.

Rep [Rows 14–31] 6 more times.

Rep Rows 14–25.

Pull-Through End

Set-up row (WS): [K1, p1] twice, k2, [p1, k1] twice, sl m, knit to next marker, sl m, [k1, p1] twice, k2, [p1, k1] twice.

Row 1 (RS): [P1, k1] twice, p2, [k1, p1] twice, sl m, [ssk, k1] 3 times, k3, [k1, k2tog] 3 times, sl m, [p1, k1] twice, p2, [k1, p1] twice—35 sts.

Row 2 and all WS rows: [K1, p1] twice, k2, [p1, k1] twice, sl m, knit to next marker, sl m, [k1, p1] twice, k2, [p1, k1] twice.

Row 3: [P1, k1] twice, p2, [k1, p1] twice, sl m, [ssk, k1] twice, k3, [k1, k2tog] twice, sl m, [p1, k1] twice, p2, [k1, p1] twice—31 sts.

Row 5: 5/5 LC-Purl Rib, knit to next marker, 5/5 RC-Purl Rib.

Rows 7 & 9: [P1, k1] twice, p2, [k1, p1] twice, knit to next marker, [p1, k1] twice, p2, [k1, p1] twice.

Row 10: Rep Row 2.

Row 11: 5/5 LC-Purl Rib, knit to next marker, 5/5 RC-Purl Rib.

Row 12: Rep Row 2.

Rep [Rows 7–12] 5 more times.

Next 4 rows: Rep Rows 7–10.

Shape End with Short Rows

Short Row Set 1: *(RS)* 5/5 LC-Purl Rib, k1, w&t; *(WS)* work in patt to end.

Short Row Set 2: Hiding wraps when you come to them, [p1, k1] twice, p2, [k1, p1] twice, k3, w&t; work in patt to end.

Short Row Set 3: [P1, k1] twice, p2, [k1, p1] twice, k5, w&t; work in patt to end.

Short Row Set 4: 5/5 LC-Purl Rib, k7; w&t; work in patt to end.

Short Row Set 5: [P1, k1] twice, p2, [k1, p1] twice, k9, w&t; work in patt to end.

Short Row Set 6: [P1, k1] twice, p2, [k1, p1] twice, k10, w&t; work in patt to end.

Next 2 rows: Rep Rows 11 & 12.

BO all sts in patt.

Finishing

Weave in ends. Block flat.

Follow instructions below for constructing bow.

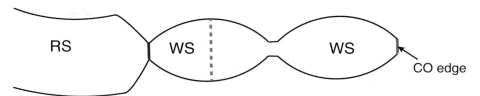

BOW CONSTRUCTION

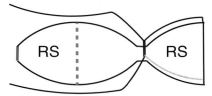

1. With right side of Body and wrong side of Bow facing up, fold bow along blue dotted line, wrong sides of Bow facing each other.

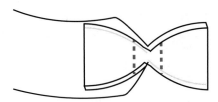

2. Fold Bow on orange dotted line, wrong sides of Bow facing each other. Sew CO edge along purple line to Body.

3. Sew through all layers along green dotted lines to form pull-through slit.

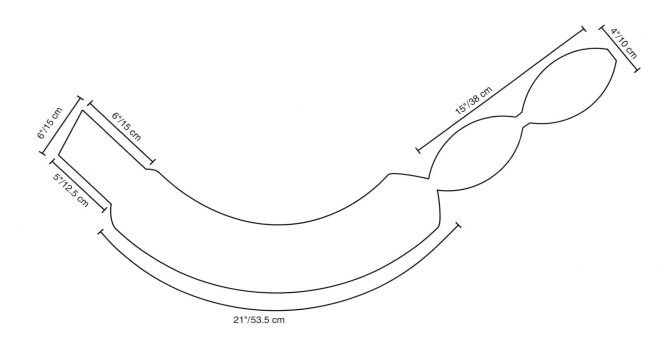

Cable Crazy

Cables are probably the quintessential stitch pattern when you think of knitting. These twists and braids of stitches can only be produced in knitted fabric. Cables are created by passing a group of stitches either in front of or behind another group of stitches, resulting in a twisted design that leaves the fabric denser and less flexible, which is ideal when you want a heavier, warmer garment. These two designs give you the option of a lighter weight fabric with the look of cables in the Duchess Wrap or a heavier Aran-style cowl in the Monarch Cable Cowl.

Duchess Wrap

The Duchess Wrap is a very simple pattern, both in stitch combinations and shaping. The faux cable stitch pattern mimics the twists and waves of traditional cables, but is actually an uncomplicated rib combination using only knit and purl stitches. "Wrap" refers to how the scarf is overlapped in order to form a V in front. A scalloped-edge cast-on forms the buttonholes, perfect for showcasing ten petite vintage buttons. The sample is shown with ten stitches on each side worked in a contrasting color to make a more pronounced scalloped edge, but it also could be worked in one color for greater simplicity of construction.

Monarch Cable Cowl

The Monarch Cable Cowl has large reversible cables that also form a scalloped edge, with seed stitch worked in between them. The ends are diagonals, formed with short-row shaping. Three large decorative pewter clasps are used as closures. The cables and the bulky yarn provide just the right amount of stiffness around the neck and drape along the front.

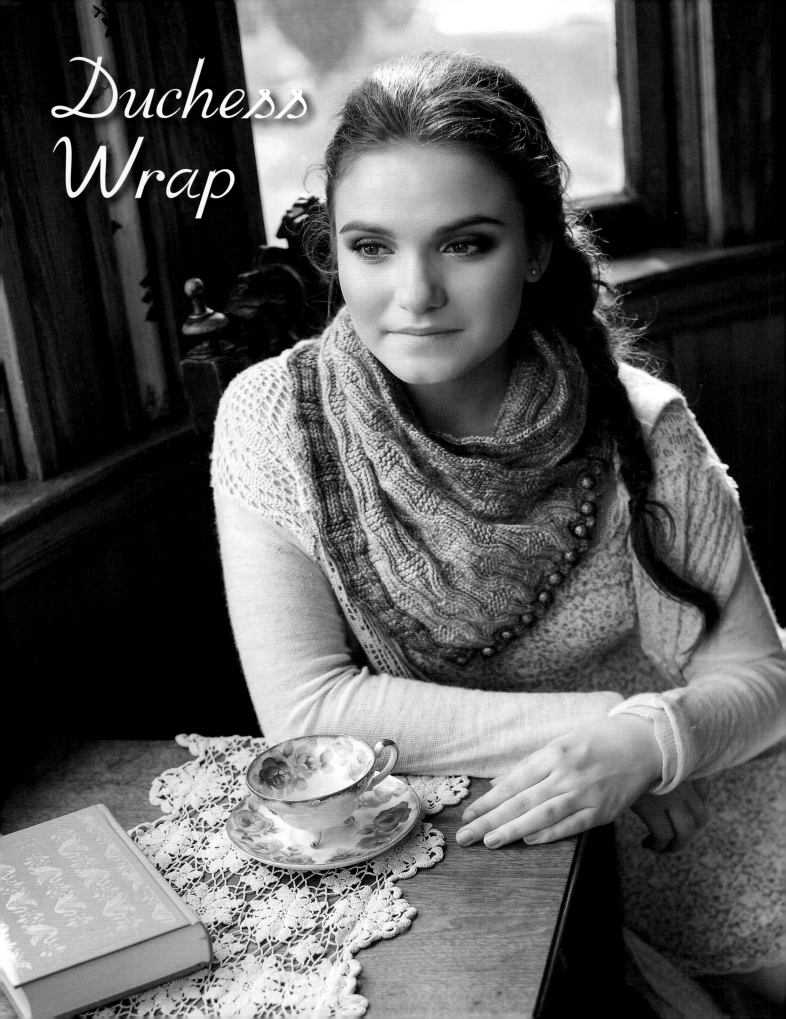

Duchess
Wrap

FINISHED MEASUREMENTS

9¾"/25 cm wide and 33½"/85 cm long

YARN

Color A: 370 yds/339 m worsted weight #4 yarn (shown in Pink Frost, Malabrigo Merino Worsted; 100% merino wool; 210 yds/192 m per 100 g skein)

Color B: 147 yds/135 m worsted weight #4 yarn (shown in Damask Rose, Malabrigo Merino Worsted; 100% merino wool; 210 yds/192 m per 100 g skein)

NEEDLES

❧ Set of US 7/4.5 mm straight knitting needles

Adjust needle size if necessary to obtain correct gauge.

NOTIONS

❧ Tapestry needle

❧ Ten ¾"/2 cm buttons

GAUGE

30 sts and 32 rows in Faux Cable Rib patt = 4"/10 cm square, lightly blocked

20 sts and 28 rows in St st = 4"/10 cm square, blocked

PATTERN NOTES

❧ The cowl is knit in one piece starting at the buttonhole edging.

❧ For contrasting color edges, the first and last 10 sts are worked with separate balls of Color B using intarsia technique. At each color change, bring the new color from below the color just used to twist them together and prevent holes.

PATTERN STITCH

Faux Cable Rib (multiple of 16 sts + 10)

Row 1 (RS): *K10, p2, k2, p2; rep from * to last 10 sts, k10.

Row 2: P2, k6, p2, *[k2, p2] twice, k6, p2; rep from * to end.

Rows 3–8: Rep [Rows 1–2] 3 times.

Row 9: K2, *p2, k2, p2, k10; rep from * to last 8 sts, [p2, k2] twice.

Row 10: [P2, k2] twice, p2, *k6, [p2, k2] twice, p2; rep from * to end.

Rows 11–16: Rep [Rows 9–10] 3 times.

Rep Rows 1–16 for patt.

Cowl

Buttonhole Edging

With B, CO 114 sts.

Row 1 (WS): Purl.

Row 2 (RS): K3, *k1, slip st just worked purlwise from RH needle back to LH needle; use RH needle to lift next 8 sts one at a time over this st and off needle, yo twice, then knit the first st again, k2; rep from * to last st, k1.

Row 3: P2, *p2tog, drop first yo of previous row, [k1, p1, k1, p1, k1] into elongated yo, p1; rep from * to last 2 sts, p2—74 sts.

Row 4: Knit.

Row 5: Purl. Do not cut B.

Body

Set-up row (RS): Working Row 1 of Faux Cable Rib patt across, work 10 sts with B; join A and cont in patt to last 10 sts; join separate ball of B and cont in patt to end.

Maintaining colors as set, cont in established Faux Cable Rib patt until piece meas approx 32½"/82.5 cm from CO edge, ending on Row 16.

Cut A and 2nd ball of B.

Edging

Row 1 (RS): With B, knit.
Row 2 (WS): Work Row 2 of Faux Cable Rib patt.
Rep [Rows 1–2] 3 times.
BO in patt.

Finishing

Weave in ends.
Block lightly, being careful to not stretch out stitch
  pattern.
Sew buttons in place, referring to schematic for
  placement.

9¾"/25 cm

← buttons

33½"/85 cm

Monarch Cable Cowl

FINISHED MEASUREMENTS

10"/25.5 cm wide and 38"/96.5 cm long

YARN

318 yds/291 m bulky weight #5 yarn (shown in Opal, O-Wool Balance Bulky; 50% organic merino wool, 50% organic cotton; 106 yds/97 m per 100 g skein)

NEEDLES

❖ Set of US 10/6 mm straight knitting needles
❖ US J–10/6 mm crochet hook (for provisional CO)
Adjust needle size if necessary to obtain correct gauge.

NOTIONS

❖ Cable needle
❖ Locking stitch markers in 2 colors (A and B)
❖ Tapestry needle
❖ 3 decorative hooks

GAUGE

14 sts and 22 rows in Seed st patt = 4"/10 cm square, blocked

PATTERN NOTES

❖ The scarf is knit in one piece, starting in the center with a provisional CO (see page 132 for a photo tutorial), then working in opposite directions.
❖ Diagonal ends are formed with short-row shaping (see page 135 for a photo tutorial).

SPECIAL STITCHES

5/5 LC-Rib: Sl 5 sts to cn and hold in front; [k1, p1], twice, k1; [k1, p1] twice, k1 from cn.
5/5 RC-Rib: Sl 5 sts to cn and hold in back; [k1, p1] twice, k1; [k1, p1] twice, k1 from cn.

PATTERN STITCHES

Side One Cable (15 sts)

Rows 1, 5, 7, 9, 13, & 15 (RS): ([K1, p1] twice, k1) 3 times.
Row 2 and all WS rows: Work sts as they present themselves.
Row 3: [K1, p1] twice, k1, 5/5 LC-Rib.
Row 11: 5/5 RC-Rib, [k1, p1] twice, k1.
Row 16: Rep Row 2.
Rep Rows 1–16 for patt.

Side Two Cable (15 sts)

Rows 1, 5, 7, 9, 13, & 15 (RS): ([K1, p1] twice, k1) 3 times.

Row 2 and all WS rows: Work sts as they present themselves.
Row 3: [K1, p1] twice, k1, 5/5 RC-Rib.
Row 11: 5/5 LC-Rib, [k1, p1] twice, k1.
Row 16: Rep Row 2.
Rep Rows 1–16 for patt.

Seed Stitch (6 sts)

Row 1 (RS): [K1, p1] 3 times.
Row 2: [P1, k1] 3 times.
Rep Rows 1–2 for patt.

Scarf

Side One

Using provisional CO, CO 57 sts.
Row 1 (RS): Working Row 1 of each patt, work Side One Cable, place marker A, work 6 sts in Seed st, work Side One Cable, place marker B, work 6 sts in Seed st, work Side One Cable.
Work in established patts until piece meas approx 11"/28 cm, ending with Cable Row 12.

Shape End with Short Rows

Short Row Set 1: *(RS)* Work in established patt to 18 sts beyond marker B, w&t; *(WS)* work in patt to end of row.
Short Row Set 2: Work in patt to 15 sts beyond marker B, w&t; work in patt to end of row.
Short Row Set 3: Work in patt to 13 sts beyond marker B, w&t; work in patt to end of row.

Short Row Set 4: Work in patt to 10 sts beyond marker B, w&t; work in patt to end of row.

Short Row Set 5: Work in patt to 8 sts beyond marker B, w&t; work in patt to end of row.

Short Row Set 6: Work in patt to 5 sts beyond marker B, w&t; work in patt to end of row.

Short Row Set 7: Work in patt to 3 sts beyond marker B, w&t; work in patt to end of row.

Short Row Set 8: Work in patt to marker B, sl m, w&t; work in patt to end of row.

Short Row Sets 9–16: Rep Short Row Sets 1–8, using marker A as your reference.

Short Row Set 17: Work 12 sts in patt, w&t; work in patt to end of row.

Short Row Set 18: Work 9 sts in patt, w&t; work in patt to end of row.

Short Row Set 19: Work 7 sts in patt, w&t; work in patt to end of row.

Short Row Set 20: Work 4 sts in patt, w&t; work in patt to end of row.

Short Row Set 21: Work 2 sts in patt, w&t; work in patt to end of row.

Next row (RS): Work in patt, hiding wraps when you come to them.

BO in patt.

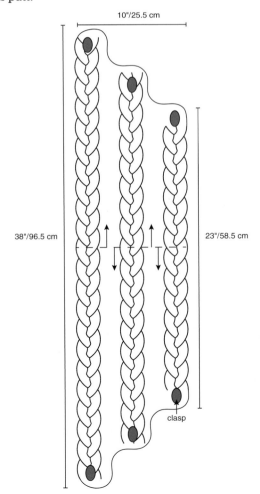

10"/25.5 cm

38"/96.5 cm

23"/58.5 cm

clasp

Side Two

Unzip provisional CO and transfer 56 live sts to needle; with RS facing, join yarn. Mark this row as center of scarf.

Row 1 (RS): Working Row 15 of Side Two Cable and Row 1 of Seed st, work Side Two Cable, work 6 sts in Seed St, place marker B, work Side Two Cable, work 5 sts in Seed St, M1, place marker A, work Side Two Cable to end—57 sts.

Work in established patts until Side Two meas approx 12"/30.5 cm from marked center row, ending with Cable Row 3.

Shape End with Short Rows

Short Row Set 1: *(WS)* Work in established patt to 18 sts beyond marker B, w&t; *(RS)* work in patt to end of row.

Short Row Set 2: Work in patt to 15 sts beyond marker B, w&t; work in patt to end of row.

Short Row Set 3: Work in patt to 13 sts beyond marker B, w&t; work in patt to end of row.

Short Row Set 4: Work in patt to 10 sts beyond marker B, w&t; work in patt to end of row.

Short Row Set 5: Work in patt to 8 sts beyond marker B, w&t; work in patt to end of row.

Short Row Set 6: Work in patt to 5 sts beyond marker B, w&t; work in patt to end of row.

Short Row Set 7: Work in patt to 3 sts beyond marker B, w&t; work in patt to end of row.

Short Row Set 8: Work in patt to marker B, sl m, w&t; work in patt to end of row.

Short Row Sets 9–16: Rep Short Row Sets 1–8, using marker A as your reference.

Short Row Set 17: Work 12 sts in patt, w&t; work in patt to end of row.

Short Row Set 18: Work 9 sts in patt, w&t; work in patt to end of row.

Short Row Set 19: Work 7 sts in patt, w&t; work in patt to end of row.

Short Row Set 20: Work 4 sts in patt, w&t; work in patt to end of row.

Short Row Set 21: Work 2 sts in patt, w&t; work in patt to end of row.

Next row (WS): Work in established patt across, hiding wraps when you come to them.

Next row: Work in patt.

BO in patt.

Finishing

Weave in ends. Block flat.

Sew on decorative hooks with tapestry needle, referring to photo for placement.

Embellished with Lace

I have a vast collection of vintage-inspired clothing, and I particularly love lace. I think a lace edging put on just about anything is a beautiful addition and lends an old-fashioned aesthetic to even the most modern clothing.

Vintage Lace Infinity Loop

The Vintage Lace Infinity Loop is knit in the round, so if you take this pattern on, get ready to tackle 280 stitches. However, the simple lace repeat and reduced number of rows makes this piece manageable, and there are quite a few rows of straight knitting or purling. The color changes in the top and bottom edges of the scarf really make the lines of the lace prominent and have the appearance of a border. A simple knit-purl checkered pattern fills the area between the two lace sections.

Leafwing

Leafwing also has delicate lace borders, but, unlike the Vintage Lace Infinity Loop whose lace border is formed by the cast-on and bind-off ends, the lace edging is knitted at the same time on both sides of the body in a contrasting color using intarsia. One lace edge is then knitted onto the body by way of a seamless connecting technique commonly used in attaching edging with square lace shawls, and attached onto the other edge. The shape is unique—sort of a V-shaped cowl and infinity scarf in one, accomplished by sewing the cast-on edge to the side of the bind-off end. Choosing a neutral color for the lace really gives it vintage appeal.

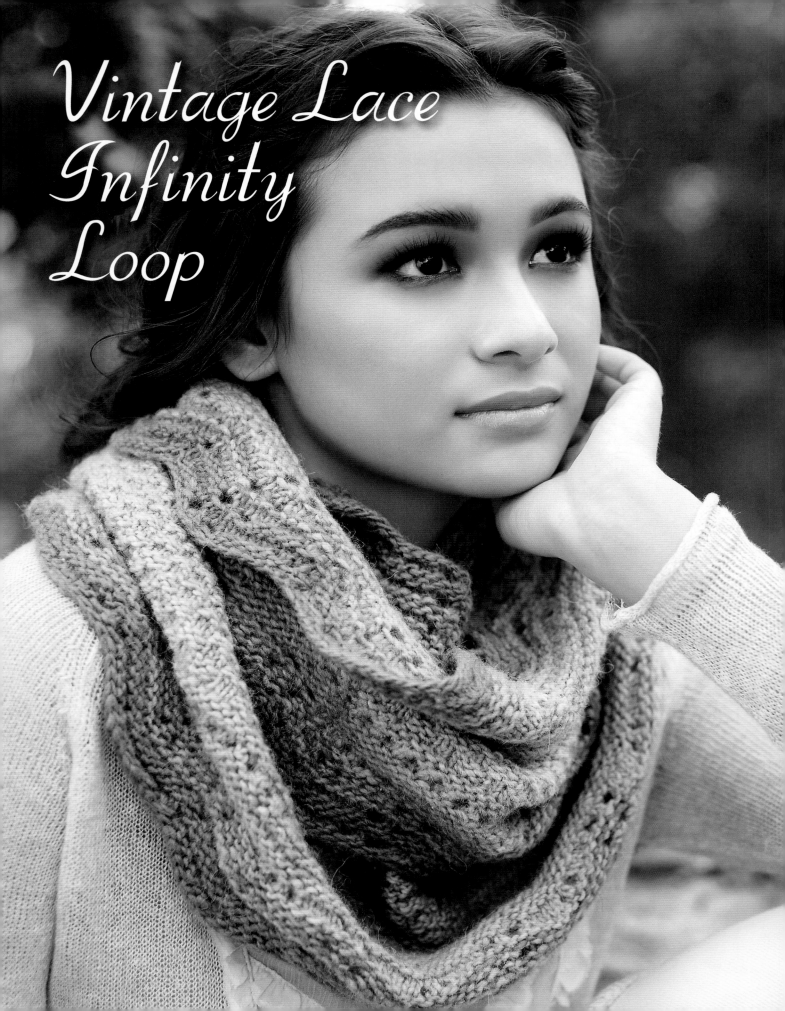

Vintage Lace
Infinity
Loop

FINISHED MEASUREMENTS

10½"/26.5 cm tall and 62"/157.5 cm circumference

YARN

Color A: 146 yds/133.5 m worsted weight #4 yarn (shown in Gray Birch, O-Wool Local; 50% organic merino wool, 50% alpaca; 240 yds/219 m per 100 g skein)

Color B: 143 yds/131 m worsted weight #4 yarn (shown in Wild Geranium, O-Wool Local; 50% organic merino wool, 50% alpaca; 240 yds/219 m per 100 g skein)

Color C: 331 yds/303 m worsted weight #4 yarn (shown in Fringetree, O-Wool Local; 50% organic merino wool, 50% alpaca; 240 yds/219 m per 100 g skein)

NEEDLES

❧ US 7/4.5 mm 32"/80 cm circular needle

Adjust needle size if necessary to obtain correct gauge.

NOTIONS

❧ Stitch marker
❧ Tapestry needle

GAUGE

18 sts and 22 rnds in Lace patt = 4"/10 cm square, blocked

20 sts and 34 rnds in Check patt = 4"/10 cm square, blocked

PATTERN NOTES

❧ The infinity scarf is knit in one piece in the round.
❧ Carry non-working yarn up at beginning of round by twisting the two yarns together.
❧ Unless instructed, do not cut non-working yarn.

SPECIAL STITCHES

Central double decrease (cdd): Sl 2 sts as if to knit 2 tog, knit 1, pass slipped sts over—2 sts dec'd.

PATTERN STITCH

Check Pattern (multiple of 4 sts)
Rnds 1–2: *K2, p2; rep from * to end.
Rnds 3–4: *P2, k2; rep from * to end.
Rep Rnds 1–4 for patt.

Infinity Scarf

Lace Edging—CO Edge (14-st rep)

With A, CO 280 sts. Mark beg of rnd and join, taking care not to twist sts.
Rnd 1: Purl.
Rnd 2: Knit.
Rnd 3: K1, ssk, yo, cdd, yo, k2tog, k3, yo, k1, yo, k2; rep from * to end.
Rnd 4: Purl.
Rnds 5–7: Rep Rnds 1–3.
Rnds 8–9: Join B; purl.

LACE EDGING - CO EDGE

LACE EDGING - BO EDGE

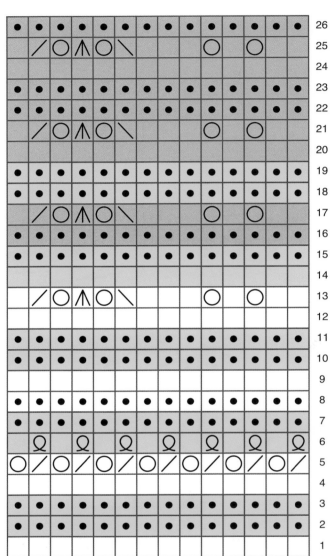

KEY

☐	Color C	Ω	K1-tbl
☐	Color B	╲	Ssk
☐	Color A	╱	K2tog
☐	Knit	⋀	Cdd
●	Purl	○	Yo

Rnds 10–11: With A, rep Rnds 2–3. Cut A.
Rnds 12–13: With B, purl.
Rnds 14–15: Join C; rep Rnds 2–3.
Rnd 16: With B, knit.
Rnd 17: Purl.
Rnd 18: With C, purl.
Rnd 19: Knit.
Rnds 20–21: With B, purl.
Rnd 22: With C, knit.
Rnd 23: *K2tog, yo; rep from * to end.
Rnd 24: With B, *k1-tbl, k1; rep from * to end.
Rnd 25: Purl. Cut B.
Rnd 26: With C, purl.
Rnd 27: Knit.

Center Section

Work Check patt until Center Section meas 4"/10 cm, ending on Rnd 2 or 4.

Lace Edging—BO Edge (14-st rep)

Rnd 1: Knit.
Rnds 2–3: Join B, purl.
Rnd 4: With C, knit.
Rnd 5: *K2tog, yo; rep from * to end.

Rnd 6: With B, *k1-tbl, k1; rep from * to end.
Rnd 7: Purl.
Rnd 8: With C, purl.
Rnd 9: Knit.
Rnds 10–11: With B, purl.
Rnd 12: With C, knit.
Rnd 13: *K2, yo, k1, yo, k3, ssk, yo, cdd, yo, k2tog, k1; rep from * to end. Cut C.
Rnd 14: With B, knit.
Rnd 15: Purl.
Rnd 16: Join A, purl.
Rnd 17: Rep Rnd 13.
Rnds 18–19: With B, purl. Cut B.
Rnd 20: With A, knit.
Rnd 21: Rep Rnd 13.
Rnds 22–23: Purl.
Rnds 24–25: Rep Rnds 20–21.
Rnd 26: Purl.
BO knitwise.

Finishing

Weave in ends.
Block.

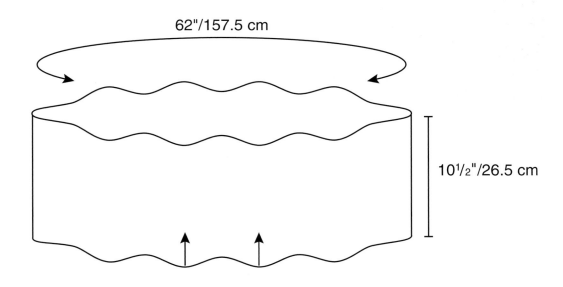

62"/157.5 cm

10½"/26.5 cm

Leafwing

FINISHED MEASUREMENTS

8½"/21.5 cm wide and 55"/140 cm long (before sewing)

YARN

Main Color (MC): 360 yds/329 m DK weight #3 yarn (shown in Celadon, Madelinetosh Tosh DK; 100% superwash merino wool; 225 yds/206 m per 100 g skein)

Contrasting Color (CC): 75 yds/69 m DK weight #3 yarn (shown in Antique Lace, Madelinetosh Tosh DK; 100% superwash merino wool; 225 yds/206 m per 100 g skein)

NEEDLES

❧ Set of US 5/3.75 mm straight knitting needles
Adjust needle size if necessary to obtain correct gauge.

NOTIONS

❧ Locking stitch markers in 2 colors (A and B)
❧ Tapestry needle

GAUGE

24 sts and 38 rows in Diamond patt = 4"/10 cm square, blocked

PATTERN NOTES

❧ The cowl is worked in one piece, with lace edges worked along with the body.
❧ The Right Lace Scallop is then worked apart from the body and attached across the top by "knitting it on," as follows: the Right Lace Scallop edging turns the right corner, is joined to the Diamond patt across the top, turns the left corner, and is finally joined to the Left Lace Scallop edging.
❧ For contrasting color edges, work Diamond patt with MC and Right and Left Lace Scallops with separate balls of CC using intarsia technique. At each color change, bring the new color from below the color just used to twist them together and prevent holes.
❧ For photo tutorials on short-row shaping and 3-needle BO, see pages 135 and 134.

PATTERN STITCHES

Diamond Pattern (multiple of 12 sts + 1)
Row 1 (RS): [P4, k5, p3] 3 times, p1.
Row 2 and all WS rows: Work the sts as they present themselves.
Row 3: [P3, k3, p1, k3, p2] 3 times, p1.
Row 5: [P2, k3, p3, k3, p1] 3 times, p1.

(continued)

Row 7: [P1, k3, p5, k3] 3 times, p1.
Row 9: [K3, p7, k2] 3 times, k1.
Row 11: [K2, p9, k1] 3 times, k1.
Row 13: Rep Row 9.
Row 15: Rep Row 7.
Row 17: Rep Row 5.
Row 19: Rep Row 3.
Row 21: Rep Row 1.
Row 23: [P5, k3, p4] 3 times, p1.
Row 24: Work as for Row 2.
Rep Rows 1–24 for patt.

Right Lace Scallop (worked over 3–8 sts)
Begin with 3 sts.
Row 1 (RS): K1, yo, ssk—3 sts.
Row 2 and all WS rows: Purl.
Row 3: K2, yo, k1—4 sts.
Row 5: K2, yo, k2—5 sts.
Row 7: K2, yo, k2tog, yo, k1—6 sts.
Row 9: K2, yo, k2tog, yo, k2—7 sts.
Row 11: K2, yo, k2tog, yo, k3—8 sts.
Row 13: K2, [yo, ssk] twice, k2—8 sts.
Row 15: K1, [ssk, yo] twice, ssk, k1—7 sts.
Row 17: K1, [ssk, yo] twice, ssk—6 sts.
Row 19: K1, ssk, yo, ssk, k1—5 sts.
Row 21: K1, ssk, yo, ssk—4 sts.
Row 23: Ssk, yo, ssk—3 sts.
Row 24: Purl.
Rep Rows 1–24 for patt.

Left Lace Scallop (worked over 3–8 sts)
Begin with 3 sts.
Row 1 (RS): K2tog, yo, k1—3 sts.
Row 2 and all WS rows: Purl.
Row 3: K1, yo, k2—4 sts.
Row 5: K2, yo, k2—5 sts.
Row 7: K1, yo, ssk, yo, k2—6 sts.
Row 9: K2, yo, ssk, yo, k2—7sts.
Row 11: K3, yo, ssk, yo, k2—8 sts.
Row 13: K2, [k2tog, yo] twice, k2—8 sts.
Row 15: K1, [k2tog, yo] twice, k2tog, k1—7 sts.
Row 17: [K2tog, yo] twice, k2tog, k1—6 sts.
Row 19: K1, k2tog, yo, k2tog, k1—5 sts.
Row 21: K2tog, yo, k2tog, k1—4 sts.
Row 23: K2tog, yo, k2tog—3 sts.
Row 24: Purl.
Rep Rows 1–24 for patt.

Cowl

Using CC, CO 3 sts, place marker B, CO 37 sts, place marker A, CO 3 sts—43 sts.
Row 1 (RS): Working Row 1 of each patt, work Right Lace Scallop to marker A; join MC and work Diamond patt to marker B; join separate ball of CC and work Left Lace Scallop to end.
Work in established patts until piece meas approx 55"/140 cm, ending with Row 8—49 sts.

Knitting on the Edging Across the Top
This is a method for attaching a border that is often used with square or rectangular shawls and involves taking one of the lace edges (in this case, the Right Lace Scallop) and knitting it separately from the body (the Diamond Pattern portion) of the cowl. The lace edge will curve to the left by working short rows to form a wedge on the RH side corner of the edging:

Turn Corner with Right Lace Scallop
Short Row Set 1 (Rows 9–10 of Right Lace Scallop patt): *(RS)* K2, yo, k2tog, yo, k1, w&t; *(WS)* purl back.
Short Row Set 2 (Rows 11–12): K2, yo, k2tog, yo, k1, w&t; purl back—8 sts rem for Right Lace Scallop.
The sts for the Right Lace Scallop will now be perpendicular to the body sts and will be attached to the Diamond patt portion as follows:

Join Lace Scallop to Top
Starting with Row 13 of Right Lace Scallop, work to last st of edging, then last st of edging will be joined to first stitch of body using an ssk as follows: sl last st of Right Lace Scallop knitwise, sl first st of Diamond patt knitwise, then k2tog tbl, resulting in the lace being attached to the body. Turn work and purl back.
Continue working Right Lace Scallop, joining last st of edging to next st from Diamond patt section using ssk. *Note: On Rows 1, 17, 21, and 23 of Right Lace Scallop, the last 2 patt sts are worked as ssk, so end those rows with sssk as follows: sl last 2 sts of Right Lace Scallop individually knitwise, sl first st of Diamond patt knitwise, then k3tog tbl.*
Continue to join Right Lace Scallop to Diamond patt section until only 1 Diamond patt st rem, ending with Row 12 of Right Lace Scallop—8 sts.
The Right Lace Scallop will now turn to the left again using short rows to complete the left corner, then the end of the Right Lace Scallop will be joined to the end of the Left Lace Scallop, closing the lace around the 3 edges of the body.

DIAMOND PATTERN

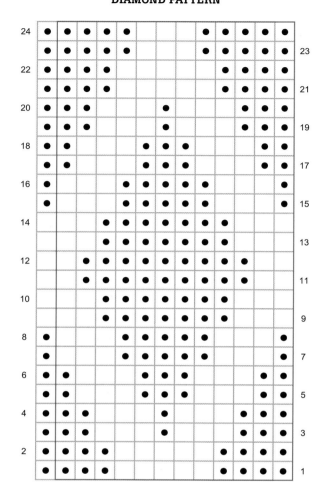

LEFT LACE SCALLOP

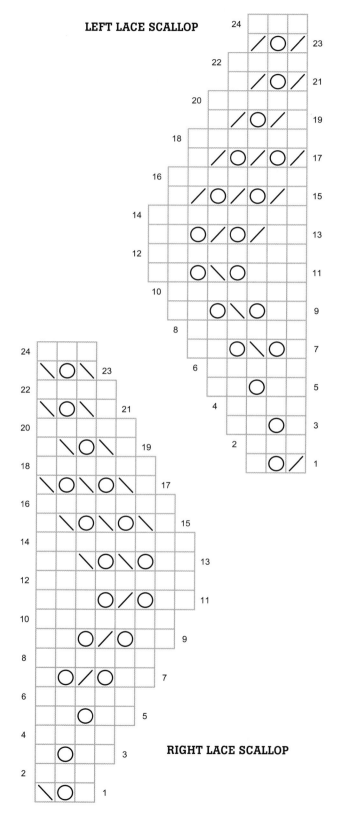

RIGHT LACE SCALLOP

KEY

□	RS: Knit WS: Purl
●	RS: Purl WS: Knit
○	Yo
╱	K2tog
╲	Ssk
▢	12-st repeat

Turn Corner with Right Lace Scallop

Short Row Set 1 (Rows 13–14): (RS) K2, [yo, ssk] twice, w&t; (WS) purl back.

Short Row Set 2 (Rows 15–16): K1, [ssk, yo] twice, ssk (hiding wrap), w&t; purl back—7 sts.

Work Row 17 of Right Lace Scallop patt to last 2 sts, sssk (hiding wrap while joining last st)—6 sts.

Using 3-needle BO, join the 6 Right Lace Scallop sts to the 6 Left Lace Scallop sts. Note: Sts can also be grafted together.

Finishing

Weave in ends. Block flat, pinning lace scallops firmly to open up.

With WS facing and allowing scalloped edge to overlap on RS, sew CO edge to top side edge as shown in schematic.

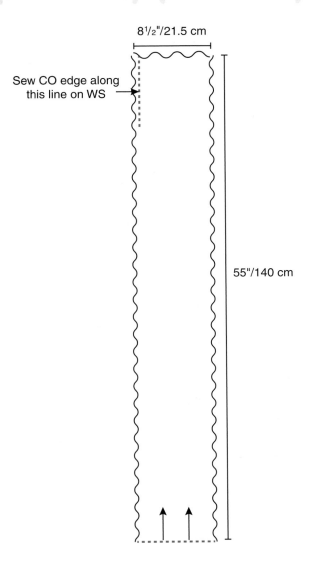

8½"/21.5 cm

Sew CO edge along this line on WS

55"/140 cm

Three– Dimensional Stripes

I love the geometric patterns in both of these pieces; they're perfect for showcasing subtle or bold yarn color combinations. The color changes are worked as stripes—one block of color is worked at a time, but the stitch patterning creates an illusion of more complex color work.

Mosaic Square Cowl

The Mosaic Square Cowl is so simple to knit, yet its texture and appearance at first glance resemble entrelac. Knit in the round, it is made with a six-stitch pattern that is repeated on every row with occasional row color changes. There are so many ways you can combine colors to achieve different looks with this piece. I chose to do an ombré effect in shades of blue on one side, continuing in just one shade of blue onto the other side, resulting in a reversible cowl that can be worn with multicolored section out or solid squares out.

Bubble Scarf

The "bubbles" in the Bubble Scarf are formed by knitting into a stitch five rows down, then dropping the corresponding stitch off the needle and letting the stitches in the four rows above that one unravel. When you pull that just-knitted stitch up, it forms a little pillow. This technique is a little more challenging than the simple stitch pattern in Mosaic Square Cowl, but once mastered, it is quick and easy. The beveled ends are shaped with short rows, but this step can be eliminated; just continue to work even and end with a straight-across bind off, leaving a squared-off edge. Using a bold contrasting color such as chartreuse for the vertical slipped stitch columns creates the look of a plaid pattern.

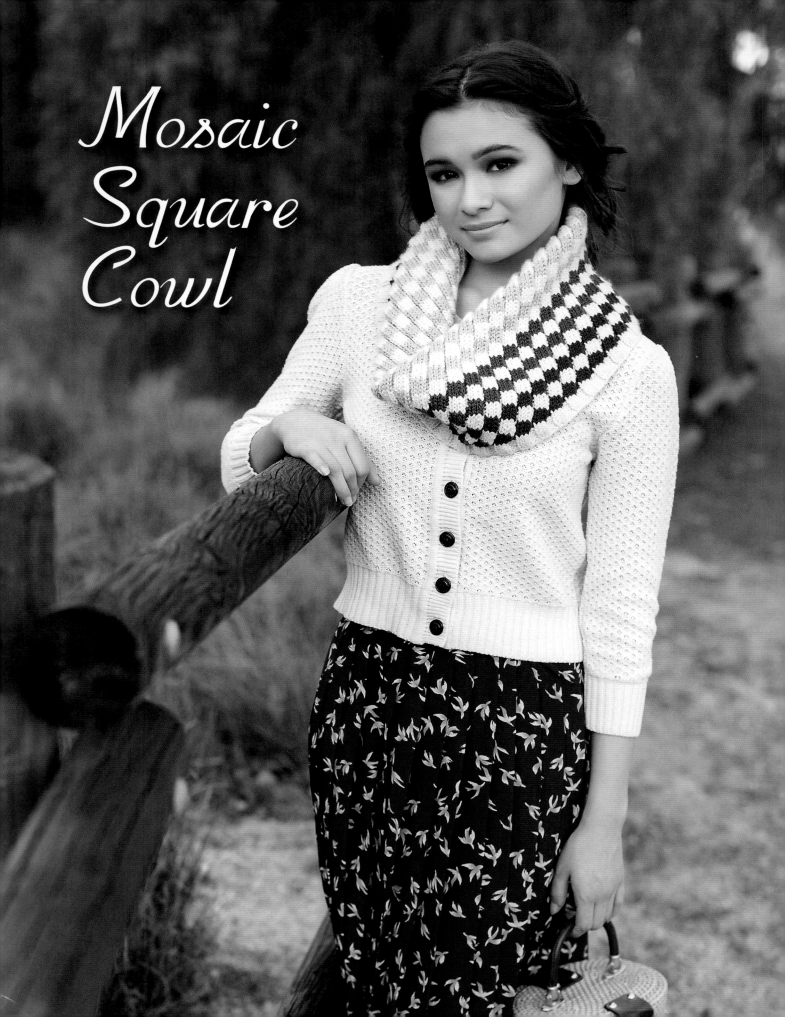

Mosaic Square Cowl

FINISHED MEASUREMENTS

12½"/32 cm tall and 30"/76 cm circumference

YARN

Color A: 258 yds/236 m worsted weight #4 yarn (shown in #1000 Heirloom White, Purl Soho Worsted Twist; 100% merino wool; 164 yds/150 m per 100 g skein)

Color B: 36 yds/33 m worsted weight #4 yarn (shown in #1580 Timeless Navy, Purl Soho Worsted Twist; 100% merino wool; 164 yds/150 m per 100 g skein)

Color C: 36 yds/33 m worsted weight #4 yarn (shown in #1540 Peacock Blue, Purl Soho Worsted Twist; 100% merino wool; 164 yds/150 m per 100 g skein)

Color D: 147 yds/135 m worsted weight #4 yarn (shown in #1520 Desert Blue, Purl Soho Worsted Twist; 100% merino wool; 164 yds/150 m per 100 g skein)

NEEDLES

⚜ US 7/4.5 mm 32"/80 cm circular needle
Adjust needle size if necessary to obtain correct gauge.

NOTIONS

⚜ Stitch marker
⚜ Tapestry needle

GAUGE

38 sts and 26 rnds in Bias Rib patt = 4"/10 cm square, measured along the diagonal, blocked
20 sts and 28 rnds in St st = 4"/10 cm square, blocked

PATTERN NOTES

⚜ The cowl is knit in one piece in the round.
⚜ Carry non-working yarn up at beginning of round by twisting the two yarns together.

PATTERN STITCH

Bias Rib (multiple of 6 sts)

Patt rnd: *K2, yo, k2, k2tog; rep from * around.

Cowl

With A, CO 216 sts. Mark beg of rnd and join, taking care not to twist sts.

Rnds 1–4: *K2, p3, k1; rep from * around.

Rnd 5: Work Bias Rib around. Do not cut A.

Rnds 6–9: With B, work Bias Rib around. Do not cut B.

Rnds 10–13: With A, work Bias Rib around. Do not cut A.

Rnds 14–21: Rep Rnds 6–13. Cut B.

Fold with inside edge out for a more subtle color combination.

Rnds 22–37: Rep Rnds 6–21, using C in place of B. Cut C.

Rnds 38–85: Rep Rnds 6–21, using D in place of B.

Rnds 86–93: Rep Rnds 6–13, using D in place of B.

Rnds 94–97: Rep Rnds 6–9, using D in place of B. Cut D.

Rnd 98: With A, rep Rnd 5.

Rnds 99–102: Rep Rnds 1–4.

BO in patt.

Finishing

Weave in ends.

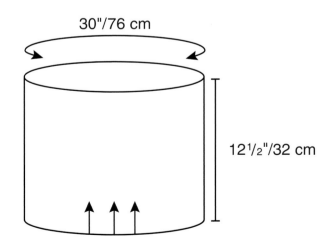

30"/76 cm

12½"/32 cm

Bubble Scarf

FINISHED MEASUREMENTS

5"/12.5 cm wide and 67"/170 cm long

YARN

Color A: 177 yds/162 m chunky weight #5 yarn (shown in #1000 Heirloom White, Purl Soho Super Soft Merino; 100% merino wool; 87 yds/79.5 m per 100 g skein)

Color B: 32 yds/30 m chunky weight #5 yarn (shown in #3010 Sea Salt, Purl Soho Super Soft Merino; 100% merino wool; 87 yds/79.5 m per 100 g skein)

Color C: 32 yds/30 m chunky weight #5 yarn (shown in #2055 Storm Gray, Purl Soho Super Soft Merino; 100% merino wool; 87 yds/79.5 m per 100 g skein)

Color D: 32 yds/30 m chunky weight #5 yarn (shown in #2040 Toasted Charcoal, Purl Soho Super Soft Merino; 100% merino wool; 87 yds/79.5 m per 100 g skein)

Color E: 65 yds/60 m chunky weight #5 yarn (shown in #1420 Extra Green, Purl Soho Super Soft Merino; 100% merino wool; 87 yds/79.5 m per 100 g skein)

NEEDLES

❋ US 11/8 mm straight needles
❋ Set of US 11/8 mm double-pointed needles
❋ US L-11/8 mm crochet hook (for provisional CO)
Adjust needle size if necessary to obtain correct gauge.

NOTIONS

❋ Tapestry needle

GAUGE

12 sts and 24 rows in Windowpane patt = 4"/10 cm square, blocked

14 sts and 24 rows in St st = 4"/10 cm, blocked

PATTERN NOTES

❋ The center section of the scarf is worked first, starting with a Provisional CO (see page 132 for a photo tutorial), then ties are worked out in opposite directions.

❋ Diagonal ends are formed with short-row shaping (see page 135 for a photo tutorial).

❋ Carry Color E up side when not being worked by twisting it with working CC yarn.

❋ Cut colors A, B, C and D (referred to generically as CC) after each color section is complete.

❋ See page 133 for a photo tutorial on 3-needle join.

PATTERN STITCHES

Windowpane Pattern (multiple of 4 sts + 3)

Rows 1 & 3 (RS): With CC, knit.

Rows 2 & 4 (WS): Purl.

Row 5: With E, k3; *insert needle from front into st 5 rows below next st (i.e., into last st worked with E), then knit into that st, letting all sts above unravel so that all strands are caught by new st; k3; rep from * to end.

Row 6: Purl.

Rep Rows 1–6 for patt.

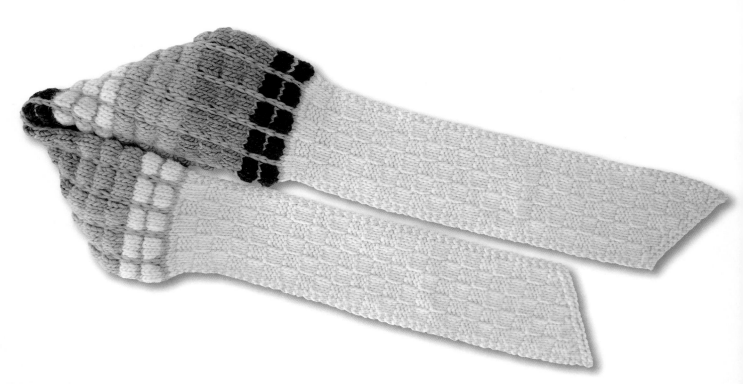

Block Pattern (19 sts)

Row 1 (RS): K2, [k3, p3] twice, k5.
Row 2 (WS): K2, [p3, k3] twice, p3, k2.
Rows 3–4: Rep Rows 1–2.
Rows 5 & 7: Rep Row 2.
Rows 6 & 8: Rep Row 1.
Rep Rows 1–8 for patt.

Scarf

Middle Section

With A and using provisional CO, CO 35 sts.
Set-up row (WS): Purl.
Row 1 (RS): Join E; knit.
Row 2: Purl.
Rows 3–14: Starting with Row 1 and using Color A for CC, work 2 reps of 6-row Windowpane patt. Cut A.
Rows 15–32: Using Color B for CC, work 3 reps of Windowpane patt. Cut B.
Rows 33–50: Using Color C for CC, work 3 reps of Windowpane patt. Cut C.
Rows 51–68: Using Color D for CC, work 3 reps of Windowpane patt. Cut D.
Rows 69–86: Using Color A for CC, work 3 reps of Windowpane patt. Cut A.
Rows 87–122: Rep Rows 15–50.
Rows 123–134: Using Color D for CC, work 2 reps of Windowpane patt. Cut D.
Row 135: With A, knit.
Row 136: Purl.

First Tie

Place first 8 sts on a dpn. Fold these sts back or inward toward WS (WS of first 8-stitch section on dpn is facing WS of first 8 sts on LH needle); hold dpn and LH needle parallel, with dpn in the back.
With A and other straight needle, using 3-needle join, [knit tog a st from the front needle with 1 from the back needle] 8 times, k3. Place last 8 sts on a dpn and fold these sts back toward WS. Holding needles parallel with dpn in back of LH needle, [knit tog a st from the front needle with 1 from the back needle] 8 times—19 sts.
Next row (WS): K2, purl to last 2 sts, k2.
Work 8-row Block patt until tie meas approx 17½"/44.5 cm, ending on a WS row.

Shape Ends with Short Rows

Maintaining established Block patt throughout, work short rows as follows:
Short Row Set 1: *(RS)* Work to last 3 sts, w&t; *(WS)* work to end of row.
Short Row Set 2: Work to last 5 sts, w&t; work to end of row.
Short Row Set 3: Work to last 7 sts, w&t; work to end of row.
Short Row Set 4: Work to last 9 sts, w&t; work to end of row.
Short Row Set 5: Work to last 11 sts, w&t; work to end of row.
Short Row Set 6: Work to last 13 sts, w&t; work to end of row.
Short Row Set 7: Work to last 15 sts, w&t; work to end of row.
Short Row Set 8: Work to last 17 sts, w&t; work to end of row.
Next row (RS): Knit across, hiding wraps when you come to them.
Next 2 rows: Knit.
BO all sts.

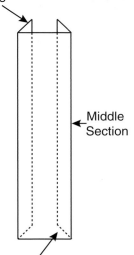

Fold first and last 8 side stitches back and knit together with center stitches.

Middle Section

Fold first 7 and last 8 side stitches back and knit together with center stitches.

Second Tie

Unzip Provisional CO; with RS facing, place last 8 sts
on a dpn, next 19 sts on a straight needle, and first 7
sts on a dpn. Fold the first 7 sts on the dpn back or
inward toward WS (WS of first 7-st section on dpn is
facing WS of first 7 sts of the 19-st section) and hold
dpn and straight needle parallel, with dpn in the
back. With A and other straight needle, using 3-
needle join, [knit tog a st from the front needle with
1 from the back needle] 7 times, k4. Fold last 8 sts
on dpn towards WS. Holding needles parallel with
dpn in back of straight needle, [knit tog a st from the
front needle with 1 from the back needle] 8 times—
19 sts.
Next row (WS): K2, purl to last 2 sts, k2.
Work 8-row Block patt until tie meas approx
17¹/₂"/44.5 cm, ending on a RS row.

Shape Ends with Short Rows
Maintaining established Block patt throughout, work
short rows as follows:
Short Row Set 1: *(WS)* Work to last 3 sts, w&t; *(RS)*
work to end of row.
Short Row Set 2: Work to last 5 sts, w&t; work to end
of row.
Short Row Set 3: Work to last 7 sts, w&t; work to end
of row.
Short Row Set 4: Work to last 9 sts, w&t; work to end
of row.
Short Row Set 5: Work to last 11 sts, w&t; work to
end of row.
Short Row Set 6: Work to last 13 sts, w&t; work to
end of row.
Short Row Set 7: Work to last 15 sts, w&t; work to
end of row.
Short Row Set 8: Work to last 17 sts, w&t; work to
end of row.
Next row (WS): Knit across, hiding wraps when you
come to them.
Next 2 rows: Knit.
BO all sts.

Finishing

Weave in ends. Block to shape.

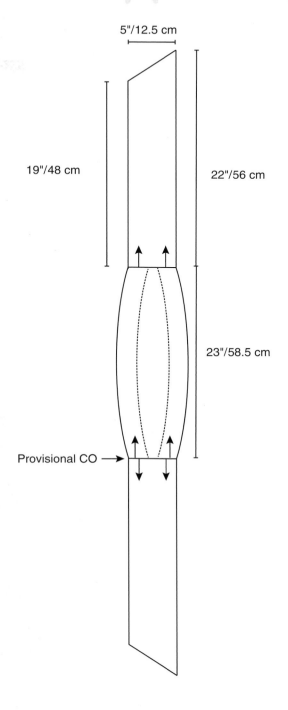

Lacy Layers

What is more pretty and feminine than layers of lace? These two scarves were inspired by the Civil War–era layered lace petticoats worn under beautiful gowns, and can be worn as dressy accessories. For both of these patterns, the lace layers are knitted separately, then the 3-needle join technique seamlessly creates tiers of lace.

Petticoat Cowl

The Petticoat Cowl, with its double lace layer trim, is a good project if you are new to three-needle techniques or if you prefer a more subtle lace embellishment. It is knit in the round, with two separate, short scalloped lace pieces joined together as one layer, and the remainder worked in a simple rib stitch pattern. The cowl is turned in and worn doubled, resembling a cowl collar on a sweater.

Baklava

Baklava is named for the rich, sweet pastry made of multiple leaves of filo dough. This scarf is equally lush, constructed of multiple tiers of lace scallops in different shades of pink. Each layer is made separately, then worked into the body of the scarf after knitting ties that are worked with reversible-cabled edges. There is a lot of detail in the design elements of this scarf, but the finished piece is a real showstopper!

Petticoat
Cowl

FINISHED MEASUREMENTS

10½"/26.5 cm tall and 23"/58.5 cm circumference

YARN

Color A: 250 yds/228.5 m DK weight #3 yarn (shown in Au Natural, Anzula Cricket; 80% superwash merino wool, 10% cashmere, 10% nylon; 250 yds/228.5 m per 100 g skein)

Color B: 44 yds/40.5 m DK weight #3 yarn (shown in Herb, Anzula Cricket; 80% superwash merino wool, 10% cashmere, 10% nylon; 250 yds/228.5 m per 100 g skein)

Color C: 20 yds/18.5 m DK weight #3 yarn (shown in Seabreeze, Anzula Cricket; 80% superwash merino wool, 10% cashmere, 10% nylon; 250 yds/228.5 m per 100 g skein)

NEEDLES

🦋 2 sets of US 4/3.5 mm 24"/61 cm circular needles

Adjust needle size if necessary to obtain correct gauge.

NOTIONS

🦋 Stitch markers
🦋 Tapestry needle

GAUGE

28 sts and 28 rnds in Lace patt = 4"/10 cm square, blocked

20 sts and 28 rnds in St st = 4"/10 cm square, blocked

PATTERN NOTES

🦋 The cowl is knit in one piece in the round.
🦋 Work Layer 1 and Layer 2 separately, then join layers together using 3-needle join (see page 133 for a photo tutorial).

Cowl

Layer 1

With A, CO 160 sts. Mark beg of rnd and join, taking care not to twist sts.

Rnd 1: Knit.
Rnd 2: Purl. Cut A.
Rnds 3–4: Join B, knit.
Rnd 5: *[K2tog] 3 times, [k1, yo] 5 times, k1, [k2tog] twice; rep from * around.
Rnd 6: Purl.
Rnds 7–14: Rep Rnds 3–6 twice.
Rnds 15–16: Knit. Cut B. Do not bind off.

Layer 2

With A and other circular needle, CO 160 sts. Mark beg of rnd and join, taking care not to twist sts.

Rnd 1: Knit.
Rnd 2: Purl. Cut A.
Rnds 3–4: Join C, knit.
Rnd 5: *[Yo, k1] 3 times, [k2tog] 5 times, [k1, yo] twice, k1; rep from * around.
Rnd 6: Purl.
Rnds 7–10: Rep Rnds 3–6. Cut C.

Join Layers

With A and using 3-needle join, join Layer 1 to Layer 2.
Next rnd: P2tog, purl to end—159 sts.

*Another way to wear the
Petticoat Cowl.*

Body

Rnd 1: *K2, p2; rep from * to last 3 sts, k2, p1.

Rnd 2: K1, p2, *k2, p2; rep from * around.

Rep Rnds 1–2 until piece meas 7½"/19 cm, ending on
   Rnd 2.

Rep [Rnd 1] 6 times.

BO in patt.

Finishing

Weave in ends.

Block to shape, pinning lace edgings firmly to open up.

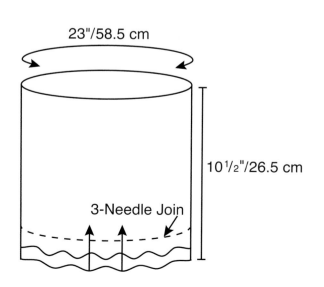

23"/58.5 cm

10½"/26.5 cm

3-Needle Join

Baklava

FINISHED MEASUREMENTS

5½"/14 cm wide x 42"/106.5 cm long

YARN

Color A: 282 yds/258 m fingering weight #1 yarn (shown in Mauve, Anzula Squishy; 80% superwash merino wool, 10% cashmere, 10% nylon; 385 yds/352 m per 115 g skein)

Color B: 53 yds/48.5 m fingering weight #1 yarn (shown in Wine, Anzula Squishy; 80% superwash merino wool, 10% cashmere, 10% nylon; 385 yds/352 m per 115 g skein)

Color C: 53 yds/48.5 m fingering weight #1 yarn (shown in Blush, Anzula Squishy; 80% superwash merino wool, 10% cashmere, 10% nylon; 385 yds/352 m per 115 g skein)

NEEDLES

❦ 2 sets of US 3/3.25 mm straight knitting needles (3 needles needed for 3-needle join and BO)
❦ US D-3/3.25 mm crochet hook (for provisional CO)
Adjust needle size if necessary to obtain correct gauge.

NOTIONS

❦ Spare circular needles or scrap yarn to use as stitch holders
❦ Locking stitch markers in 2 colors (A and B)
❦ Cable needle
❦ Tapestry needle

GAUGE

34 sts and 38 rows in 1x1 Rib = 4"/10 cm square, lightly blocked

PATTERN NOTES

❦ Ties are reversible with reversible-cabled edges.
❦ Ties are knit from pointed end up.
❦ Individual scallops are made first, then attached to scarf as you knit, using 3-needle join (see page 133 for a photo tutorial).
❦ For photo tutorials for provisional CO, short-row shaping, and 3-needle BO, see pages 132, 135, and 134.

SPECIAL STITCHES

5/5 LC-Rib: Sl 5 sts to cn and hold in front; [k1, p1], twice, k1; [k1, p1] twice, k1 from cn.
5/5 RC-Rib: Sl 5 sts to cn and hold in back; [k1, p1] twice, k1; [k1, p1] twice, k1 from cn.
Cluster (CL): Sl number of sts indicated to cn; wrap yarn clockwise 3 times around sts on cn; purl sts from cn.

PATTERN STITCHES

Single Scallop (worked over 24–29 sts)
CO 24 sts.
Row 1 (RS): K1, yo, k23—25 sts.
Row 2: P3, [k3, p1] 4 times, k3, p3.
Row 3: K2, yo, [k1, p3] 5 times, k1, yo, k2—27 sts.
Rows 4, 6, & 8: Work the sts as they present themselves, purling all yo's.
Row 5: K2, yo, k1, yo, [ssk, p2] 5 times, [k1, yo] twice, k2—26 sts.

(continued)

Row 7: K2, [yo, k1] 3 times, yo, [ssk, p1] 5 times, [k1, yo] 4 times, k2—29 sts.

Row 9: K9, ssk 5 times, k10—24 sts.

Row 10: P9, CL6, p9.

Row 11: Knit.

Row 12: Purl.

Cut yarn and put sts on holder or scrap yarn.

Double Scallop (worked over 45–55 sts)

CO 45 sts.

Row 1 (RS): K1, yo, k21, yo, k23—47 sts.

Row 2: *P3, [k3, p1] 4 times, k3; rep from * once, p3.

Row 3: K2, yo, [k1, p3] 5 times, [k1, yo] twice, [k1, p3] 5 times, k1, yo, k2—51 sts.

Rows 4, 6, & 8: Work the sts as they present themselves, purling all yo's.

Row 5: K2, yo, k1, yo, [ssk, p2] 5 times, [k1, yo] 4 times, [ssk, p2] 5 times, [k1, yo] twice, k2—49 sts.

Row 7: K2, [yo, k1] 3 times, yo, [ssk, p1] 5 times, [k1, yo] 8 times, [ssk, p1] 5 times, [k1, yo] 4 times, k2—55 sts.

Row 9: K9, ssk 5 times, k16, ssk 5 times, k10—45 sts.

Row 10: P9, CL6, p15, CL6, p9.

Row 11: Knit.

Row 12: Purl.

Cut yarn and put sts on holder or scrap yarn.

Split Scallop (worked over 45–55 sts)

CO 45 sts.

Row 1 (RS): K10, yo, k21, yo, k14—47 sts.

Row 2: P2, [k3, p1] twice, k3, p3, [k3, p1] 4 times, k3, p3, k3, p1, k3, p2.

Row 3: K2, [p3, k1] twice, yo, k1, yo, [k1, p3] 5 times, [k1, yo] twice, [k1, p3] 3 times, k2—51 sts.

Rows 4, 6, & 8: Work the sts as they present themselves, purling all yo's.

Row 5: K1, *[ssk, p2] twice, [k1, yo] 4 times, [ssk, p2] 3 times; rep from * once, k2—49 sts.

Row 7: K1, *[ssk, p1] twice, [k1, yo] 8 times, [ssk, p1] 3 times; rep from * once, k2—55 sts.

Row 9: K1, ssk twice, k16, ssk 5 times, k16, ssk 3 times, k2—45 sts.

Row 10: CL5, p15, CL6, p15, CL4.

Row 11: Knit.

Row 12: Purl.

Cut yarn and put sts on holder or scrap yarn.

Tie

With A, make 2 Double Scallops and 2 Split Scallops.

With B, make 1 Single Scallop, 2 Double Scallops, and 2 Split Scallops.

With C, make 1 Single Scallop, 2 Double Scallops, and 2 Split Scallops.

Block all scallops, pinning firmly to open up lace.

Right-Hand Side

With A, CO 23 sts, place marker A, CO 1 st, place marker B, CO 23 sts—47 sts.

Set-up row (WS): [P1, k1] twice, p2, *k1, p1; rep from * to last 5 sts, [p1, k1] twice, p1.

Short Row Set 1: Working sts as they present themselves throughout (knitting the knit sts and purling the purl sts), *(RS)* work to 1 st past marker B, w&t; *(WS)* work to 1 st past marker A, w&t.

Short Row Set 2: Work in patt to 3 sts past marker B, w&t; work to 3 sts past marker A, w&t, hiding wraps when you come to them.

Short Row Set 3: Work in patt to 5 sts past marker B, w&t; work to 5 sts past marker A, w&t.

Short Row Set 4: Work in patt to 7 sts past marker B, w&t; work to 7 sts past marker A, w&t.

Short Row Set 5: Work in patt to 9 sts past marker B, w&t; work to 9 sts past marker A, w&t.

Short Row Set 6: Work in patt to 11 sts past marker B, w&t; work to 11 sts past marker A, w&t.

Remove markers.

Maintaining patt, work 2 rows even.

Cable Twist row (RS): 5/5 LC-Rib, work in patt to last 10 sts, 5/5 RC-Rib.

Maintaining patt, rep Cable Twist row every 6th row until piece meas 10"/25.5 cm from center point of CO edge, ending on a WS row.

Shape End

Note: Maintain Cable Twists at each edge as established.

Row 1 (Dec row, RS): Work 11 sts in patt, ssk, work to last 13 sts, k2tog, work to end—2 sts dec'd.

Rows 2 & 4: Work sts as they present themselves.

Row 3 (Dec row): Work 10 sts in patt, ssp, work to last 12 sts, p2tog, work to end—2 sts dec'd.

Rep Rows 1–4 until 25 sts rem, ending on Row 1.

Next row (WS): P12, p2tog, p11—24 sts.

Scalloped Center

Worked in A. Attach scallops in color order shown on schematic.

Rows 1 & 3 (RS): Knit.

Row 2 and all WS rows: K2 (selvedge sts), purl to last 2 sts, k2 (selvedge sts).

Row 5: Transfer Single Scallop to a spare needle and hold in front of scarf base with RS of both pieces facing. Work pieces tog using 3-needle join.

Row 7 (Inc row): [K1, M1R] twice, knit to last 2 sts, [M1L, k1] twice—4 sts inc'd.

Rows 9, 11, &13: Rep Row 7—40 sts after Row 13.

Row 15: [K1, M1R] twice, [k18, M1L] twice, k1, M1L, k1—45 sts.

Row 17: Transfer Double Scallop to a spare needle and hold in front of scarf base with RS of both pieces facing. Work pieces tog using 3-needle join.

Rows 19, 21, 23, & 25: Knit.

Row 27: Transfer Split Scallop to a spare needle and hold in front of scarf base with RS of both pieces facing. Work pieces tog using 3-needle join.

Rows 29, 31, 33, & 35: Knit.

Rep Rows 17–35 once, then work Rows 17–27.

Next row (WS): Rep Row 2.

Transfer sts to a spare needle or scrap yarn; cut yarn.

Left-Hand Side

Work same as Right-Hand Side, but leave sts on needle and do not cut yarn. For Scalloped Center, attach scallops in color order shown on schematic for Left-Hand Side.

Finishing

Join the two sides using 3-needle BO.
Block lightly to shape.

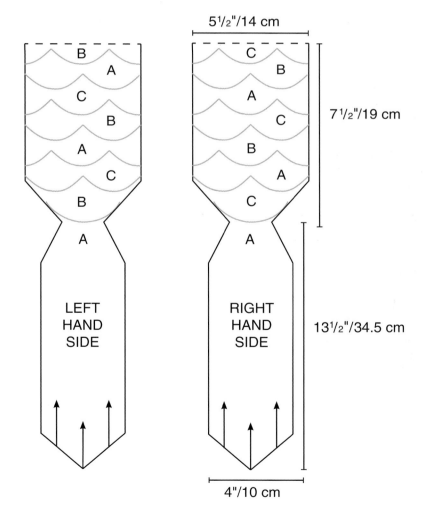

Twists & Turns

Stranding is a technique I developed that involves taking a piece of knitted fabric, dividing the stitches into sections, then knitting them separately. Those sections are either braided or left straight, and then all the stitches are joined again to form a solid knitted fabric. The strands provide interesting layers of texture, creating a luscious, enveloping effect, especially when the scarf is wrapped twice around the neck.

Challah Infinity Scarf

The Challah Infinity Scarf is one of my very first designs, and its texture reminds me of the braided bread it takes its name from. This is a very simple pattern—the strands are composed of 2x2 rib stitch and seed stitch, so the knitter only needs knowledge of knit and purl stitches. The stranding construction involves a little finessing, but I have provided some illustrations that will hopefully make that easy to maneuver.

Triple Plait

Triple Plait is also a stranded infinity scarf, but this time the strands are reversible cables that form individual plaits or braids. Unlike Challah, the knitted fabric and the strands are in separate sections. The knitted fabric is a mesh lace, so as to not make the scarf too cumbersome, since it is worked in a bulky weight yarn.

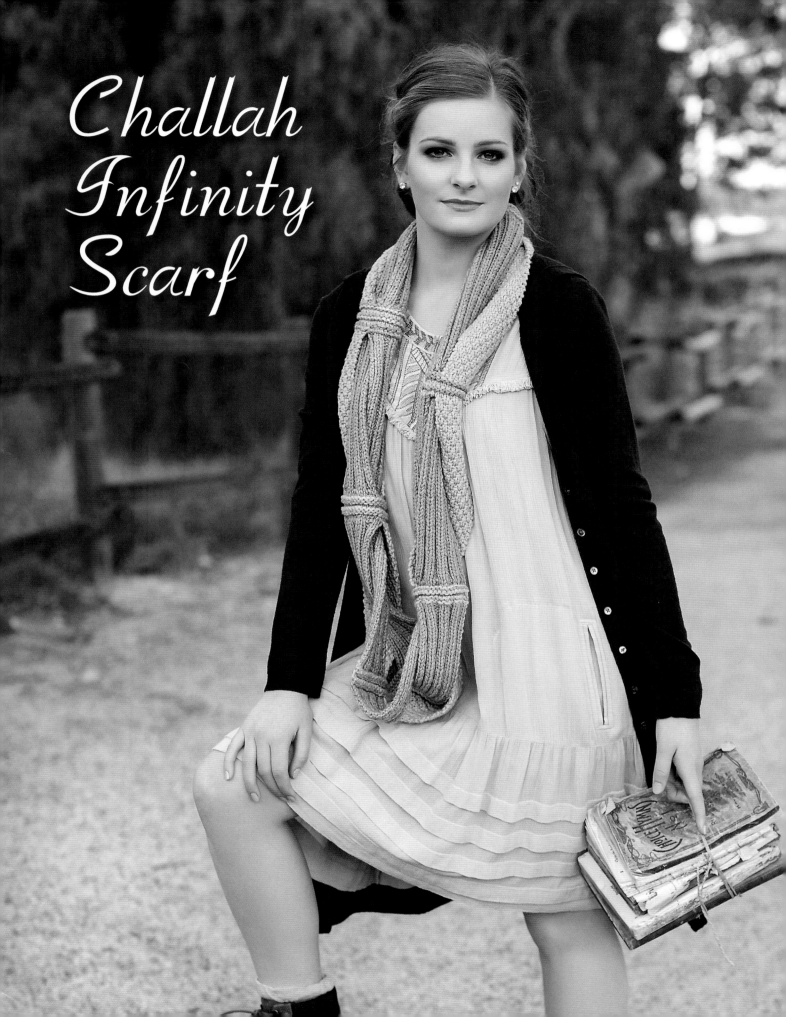

Challah Infinity Scarf

FINISHED MEASUREMENTS

8"/20.5 cm wide and 57"/145 cm long

YARN

Each of these colors is worked with 2 strands held together to form a chunky weight yarn; the overall required yardage for each takes that into account.

Color A: 308 yds/282 m worsted weight #4 yarn (shown in Seasmoke, Swans Island Pure Blends Worsted; 85% organic merino wool, 15% alpaca; 250 yds/229 m per 100 g skein)

Color B: 308 yds/282 m worsted weight #4 yarn (shown in Oyster, Swans Island Natural Colors Worsted; 100% organic merino wool; 250 yds/229 m per 100 g skein)

Color C: 295 yds/270 m (shown in Vintage Lilac, Swans Island Natural Colors Worsted; 100% organic merino wool; 250 yds/229 m per 100 g skein)

NEEDLES

* US 9/5.5 mm circular knitting needle (to access sts from both ends)

Adjust needle size if necessary to obtain correct gauge.

NOTIONS

* 2 stitch holders
* Tapestry needle

GAUGE

With 2 strands of yarn held together, 18 sts and 28 rows in Moss st = 4"/10 cm square, blocked

With 2 strands of yarn held together, 15 sts and 20 rows in St st = 4"/10 cm square, blocked

PATTERN NOTES

* The scarf is worked in one piece starting with the Beginning Section Border, followed by 6 Braided Sections, and ending with the End Section Border.
* Each of the 6 Braided Sections is worked by separating the stitches into 3 strips that are worked individually. The 3 strips are braided and then all stitches are placed back onto the needle to work the Mid-Section Join.
* Two strands of the same color yarn are held together throughout the pattern.
* Carry non-working yarn up the side of the Mid-Section Join by twisting the 2 yarns together.

PATTERN STITCHES

2x2 Rib (multiple of 4 sts + 2)

Row 1 (RS): *K2, p2; rep from * to last 2 sts, k2.
Row 2 (WS): *P2, k2; rep from * to last 2 sts, p2.
Rep Rows 1–2 for patt.

Moss Stitch (multiple of 2 sts)

Row 1 (RS) & Row 2 (WS): *K1, p1; rep from * to end.
Rows 3–4: *P1, k1; rep from * to end.
Rep Rows 1–4 for patt.

Scarf

Beginning Section Border

With A, CO 44 sts.
Row 1 (RS): Knit.
Row 2 (WS): Purl.
Row 3: Join B, purl.
Row 4: Knit. Cut B.
Row 5: With A, knit.
Row 6: Purl. Cut A.

Braided Section 1

Separate sts as follows: Transfer last 14 sts to stitch holder for Strip A; transfer middle 12 sts to separate stitch holder for Strip B; 18 sts remain on needle for Strip C.

Strip C (with C, worked over 18 sts)

With RS facing, join C.
Work 2x2 Rib patt until Strip C meas 8"/20.5 cm, ending on a WS row.
Cut C. Transfer sts to holder.

Strip B (worked with B over 12 sts)

Transfer sts for Strip B to needle. With RS facing, join B.
Work Moss st patt until Strip B meas 8½"/21.5 cm, ending on a WS row.
Cut B. Transfer sts to holder.

Strip A (worked with A over 14 sts)

Transfer sts for Strip A to needle. With RS facing, join A.
Work 2x2 Rib patt until Strip A meas 8"/20.5 cm, ending on a WS row.
Do not cut A. Transfer sts to holder.
Braid the 3 strips as shown in diagram, being careful to not twist strips (keep RS up).

Mid-Section Join

Rejoin the 3 strips by transferring all sts to working needle.
Row 1 (RS): With A, knit.
Row 2 (WS): Purl.
Row 3: Join B, purl.
Row 4: Knit.
Row 5: With A, knit.
Row 6: Purl.
Row 7: With B, purl.
Row 8: Knit. Cut B.
Row 9: With A, knit.
Row 10: Purl. Do not cut A.

Braided Section 2

Separate sts as follows: Transfer last 18 sts to stitch holder for Strip C; transfer middle 12 sts to separate stitch holder for Strip B; 14 sts remain on needle for Strip A.
Rep Braided Section 1 instructions for Strips A, B, and C, except on Strip A, cut yarn at end of strip.
When braiding strips, alternate direction of middle Strip B with each section (see diagram).
Rep Mid-Section Join, joining A on Row 1.

Braided Sections 3–6

Work 4 more Braided Sections, alternating Braided Section 1 and Braided Section 2 and connecting the braided sections with the Mid-Section Join. After braiding the last (6th) section, do not work a Mid-Section Join.

End Section Border

Rejoin 3 strips on needle, then rep Rows 1–4 of Beginning Section Border.
BO all sts.

Finishing

With RS facing, sew CO and BO ends together.

BRAIDING THE STRIP

Strip C
Strip B
Strip A

Braided Section 1 | Braided Section 2

Triple
Plait

FINISHED MEASUREMENTS

8"/20.5 cm wide and 57"/145 cm long

YARN

448 yds/410 m chunky weight #5 yarn (shown in #860 Smoke Heather, Cascade Yarns 128 Superwash; 100% superwash merino wool; 128 yds/117 m per 100 g skein)

NEEDLES

❧ 2 sets of US 10/6 mm straight knitting needles
❧ US J-10/6 mm crochet hook (for provisional CO)
Adjust needle size if necessary to obtain correct gauge.

NOTIONS

❧ 2 stitch holders
❧ Cable needle
❧ Locking stitch markers
❧ Tapestry needle

GAUGE

14 sts and 19 rows in St st = 4"/10 cm square, blocked

PATTERN NOTES

❧ The scarf is knit in one piece starting with a provisional CO (see page 132 for a photo tutorial).
❧ After the main scarf fabric is complete, the piece is divided into three separate cable "strands" that continue from the main fabric; the ends of the strands are attached to the cast-on end of the main fabric using 3-needle BO (see page 134 for a photo tutorial).
❧ The scarf is blocked with the stitches still on the needle and stitch holders; it's much more difficult to block it after binding off.

SPECIAL STITCHES

3/3 LC-Rib: Slip 3 sts to cn and hold in front; k1, p1, k1; k1, p1, k1 from cn.

3/3 RC-Rib: Slip 3 sts to cn and hold in back; k1, p1, k1; k1, p1, k1 from cn.

5/5 LC-Rib: Slip 5 sts to cn and hold in front; [k1, p1] twice, k1; [k1, p1] twice, k1 from cn.

5/5 RC-Rib: Slip 5 sts to cn and hold in back; [k1, p1] twice, k1; [k1, p1] twice, k1 from cn.

PATTERN STITCHES

Note: Charts are also provided for stitch patterns.

Small Cable (12 sts)

Row 1 and all WS rows: P1, [k1, p2] 3 times, k1, p1.
Row 2 (RS): 3/3 RC-Rib, 3/3 LC-Rib.
Row 4: K1, [p1, k2] 3 times, p1, k1.
Row 6: 3/3 LC-Rib, 3/3 RC-Rib.
Row 8: Rep Row 4.
Rep Rows 1–8 for patt.

Large Cable (20 sts)

Row 1 and all WS rows: P1, [k1, p1, k1, p2] 3 times, [k1, p1] twice.
Rows 2, 6, 8, 10, & 14 (RS): K1, [p1, k1, p1, k2] 3 times, [p1, k1] twice.
Row 4: 5/5 RC-Rib, 5/5 LC-Rib.
Row 12: 5/5 LC-Rib, 5/5 RC-Rib.
Row 16: Rep Row 2.
Rep Rows 1–16 for patt.

Small Cable Strand (12 sts)

Rows 1 & 3 (WS): P1, [k1, p2] 3 times, k1, p1.
Row 2 (RS): 3/3 RC-Rib, 3/3 LC-Rib.
Row 4: K1, [p1, k2] 3 times, p1, k1.
Rep Rows 1–4 for patt.

Large Cable Strand (20 sts)

Row 1 and all WS rows: P1, [k1, p1, k1, p2] 3 times, [k1, p1] twice.
Rows 2 & 6 (RS): K1, [p1, k1, p1, k2] 3 times, [p1, k1] twice.
Row 4: 5/5 RC-Rib, 5/5 LC-Rib.
Row 8: Rep Row 2.
Rep Rows 1–8 for patt.

Mesh Lace (8 sts)

Row 1 (WS): P3, k1, p4.
Row 2 (RS): K2tog, 2yo, [k2tog] twice, 2yo, k2tog.
Row 3: P1, [k1, p1] in double yo, p2, [k1, p1] in double yo, p1.
Row 4: K2, k2tog, 2yo, k2tog, k2.
Row 5: P3, [k1, p1] in double yo, p3.
Rows 6–8: Rep Rows 2–4.
Rep Rows 5–8 for patt.

LARGE CABLE

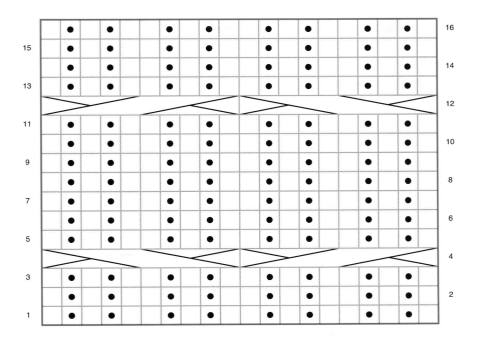

LARGE CABLE STRAND

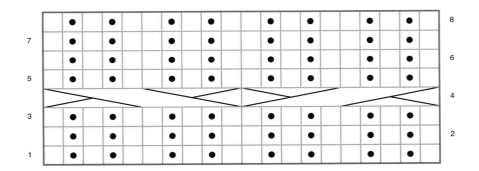

KEY

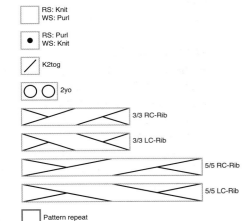

RS: Knit
WS: Purl

RS: Purl
WS: Knit

K2tog

2yo

3/3 RC-Rib

3/3 LC-Rib

5/5 RC-Rib

5/5 LC-Rib

Pattern repeat

MESH LACE

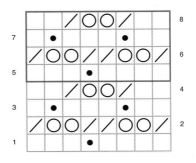

SMALL CABLE

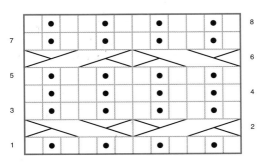

SMALL CABLE STRAND

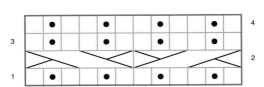

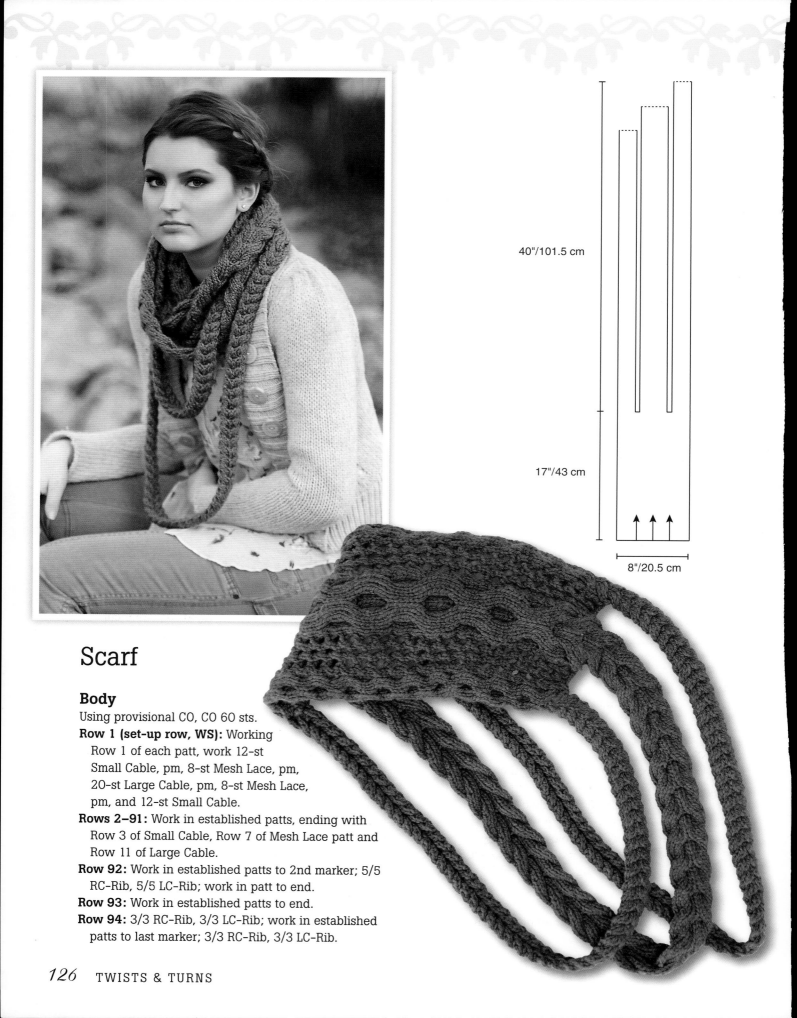

40"/101.5 cm

17"/43 cm

8"/20.5 cm

Scarf

Body

Using provisional CO, CO 60 sts.

Row 1 (set-up row, WS): Working
Row 1 of each patt, work 12-st
Small Cable, pm, 8-st Mesh Lace, pm,
20-st Large Cable, pm, 8-st Mesh Lace,
pm, and 12-st Small Cable.

Rows 2–91: Work in established patts, ending with
Row 3 of Small Cable, Row 7 of Mesh Lace patt and
Row 11 of Large Cable.

Row 92: Work in established patts to 2nd marker; 5/5
RC-Rib, 5/5 LC-Rib; work in patt to end.

Row 93: Work in established patts to end.

Row 94: 3/3 RC-Rib, 3/3 LC-Rib; work in established
patts to last marker; 3/3 RC-Rib, 3/3 LC-Rib.

Alternate ways to wear Triple Plait.

Row 95: Work in established patts.

Row 96: BO Lace Mesh sections as follows: removing markers, [work in established patt to marker; BO 6 sts, k2tog *(note: the last bound-off st is passed over the k2tog)*] twice, work in established patt to end.

Do not cut yarn.

Transfer first 12 sts onto other needle and place center 20 sts and last 12 sts on separate st holders.

Strands

With WS facing, using working yarn and starting with Row 1, work Small Cable Strand patt until piece meas approx 40"/101.5 cm, ending with Row 3.

Place sts on a st holder. Cut yarn.

Place center 20 sts on a needle and rejoin yarn.

With WS facing, starting with Row 1, work Large Cable Strand patt until piece meas approx 37"/94 cm, ending with Row 7.

Place sts on a st holder. Cut yarn.

Place final 12 sts on a needle and rejoin yarn.

With WS facing, starting with Row 1, work Small Cable Strand patt until piece meas approx 34"/86.5 cm, ending with Row 3.

Do not cut yarn.

Finishing

Block flat, with the scarf still on needle and stitch holders.

Unzip provisional CO and transfer 59 live sts to a separate needle.

Transfer cable strand sts from holders to the needle holding last cable strand worked; maintain order of cables and take care not to twist strands.

BO and join Body sts to cable-strand sts using 3-needle BO as follows: With RS facing each other, using 3-needle BO and working yarn from last cable strand worked, BO first 12 sts; BO next 8 Body sts; using 3-needle BO, BO next 20 sts; BO 7 Body sts; using 3-needle BO, BO last 12 sts.

Weave in ends.

How to Read My Patterns

Every designer has a unique way of presenting their patterns. I have developed this format over the years that I have been designing in response to feedback I have gotten from knitters.

I do not assign Level of Difficulty designations for any of my patterns. I believe that the protocols for what labels a pattern as "beginner," "intermediate," or "advanced" are a little arbitrary and may intimidate knitters from attempting a pattern that is simple but includes one technique that qualifies it otherwise. Even as an experienced knitter, I occasionally come across skills that are new to me, but once practiced and mastered, they become manageable.

Now with that being said, none of my patterns would qualify at the beginner level. In order to achieve interesting texture and embellishment details, there is a certain level of complexity involved. I encourage you to learn any new techniques that may be making you hesitate to take on a garment, and you will hopefully find that the project will become straightforward. I have also included photo tutorials on those techniques I feel require more explanation than written instruction can provide.

Finished Measurements

These are the measurements of the garment taken after blocking. For more complete measurements, refer to the schematic provided for each project. Remember also that all measurements given within the pattern as you work are blocked measurements as well. For example, if a pattern states "Work until piece meas 10"/25.5 cm," this measurement pertains to a blocked knitted fabric. So if your blocked row gauge is 7 rows per inch/2.5 cm, but unblocked gauge is 8 rows per inch, you would work 70 rows, even though your piece will measure out at 8.75"/22.25 cm unblocked. For this example, your unblocked measurement would be seven eighths of the blocked measurement you are trying to achieve, dividing your blocked gauge by your unblocked gauge. If this is too confusing, you can also work to an inch or

two under the measurement required and block your piece while on the needles. For longer garments such as scarves and infinity loops, the measurements are not crucial; but for ascot-style pieces, the length is important to fit—nobody wants to be choked by a too-tight ascot or sport a droopy, awkward one that is too long. Each pattern includes a schematic that should be referenced for finished dimensions.

Yarn

For each project, I tell you how many yards are required (and for each yarn, if there are multiple colors), so you'll be able to figure out how many skeins you need, no matter what yarns you choose. The particular yarns and colors I used for the project are listed, including their weight, fiber content, and how many yards/meters are in each skein.

Yarn Substitutions

If you decide to use an alternate yarn, there are a number of factors to consider to ensure success. The gauge needs to be within 1 to 2 stitches (taken from a 4"/10 cm swatch) of the gauge listed for the pattern. However, the weight of the yarn is also an important consideration. Calculate the yards per gram for both the yarn used and for the substitution yarn by dividing the yards per skein by the grams per skein. If there is a large difference (more than 10%), then the finished product may have a different drape than the sample shown in the book, which is a problem for patterns that are dependent on a certain degree of substance, like those with ruffles. Also it's important that the substitute yarn have a fiber content that behaves similarly to that of the original yarns used, as different fibers have varying densities that will perform differently in patterns regardless of the gauge. For example, a wool yarn tends to have a lot of body, whereas a cotton or hemp yarn typically will not, and so would not be a good substitution.

Needles

These are the needle sizes and types used in production of the samples. However, if your gauge does not match the pattern gauge listed (see below for more on that), then you will need to adjust your needle size to obtain the appropriate gauge. If your swatch ends up being too large, move down a needle size, and vice versa. Some patterns have circular needles listed even though the piece is not knitted in the round. This is because either a longer needle is required to accommodate the number of stitches being worked, or because you will need to access the knitting from both ends of the needle. In this circumstance, you could use straight needles and transfer the stitches over to the second needle in order to work from the other end. If there is not a large number of stitches being worked, you could also use a double-pointed needle.

Notions

These supplies include such things as stitch markers and holders, tapestry needles, and buttons and other closures.

Gauge

This is the gauge you need to match in order for the finished garment to correspond to the dimensions on the schematic. The gauge is always given for blocked, knitted fabric. Please take the time to knit a gauge swatch. Even though these are scarves and the fit need not be as exact as for a sweater, if you are too far off track, your finished piece may look disproportional. Also, the swatch is where you will determine if the stitches look pleasing. For example, if you need to go up one or more needle sizes in order to achieve the listed gauge, but there are big holes in the stitches caused by the looseness of the fabric, then that yarn is not a good match for the project. Make a good size swatch (I usually make a 6"/15.5 cm square swatch) and take the time to block it before measuring it.

Pattern Notes

This is where any special construction notes are given, such as how the piece is worked, i.e., from the top down, from the center out starting with a provisional cast-on, etc. Some patterns have special selvedge instructions such as "slip first stitch of every row with

yarn in front." Be sure to check for any Pattern Notes before starting the project.

Special Stitches

This is a list of the special stitches used in the pattern and how to execute them.

Pattern Stitches

This is where you will find stitch patterns that are used as a repeat within the instructions. If there is a chart included with the pattern, this is where you will find the row-by-row instructions listed for the corresponding chart. Charts are read from the bottom up and from right-to-left on right-side rows. Wrong-side rows are read from left-to-right. The symbols on the chart represent the pattern as you are looking at it from the right side. If knitting in the round, every row is a right-side row. If knitting flat, the symbols need to be reinterpreted for the wrong side; for example, a knit symbol will be purled and a purl symbol will be knit.

Finishing

When sewing on buttons or hooks, I always try to use the project yarn and a tapestry needle. Sewing thread has a tendency to cut through yarn over time. However, occasionally it will be necessary to use a sewing needle and thread if the holes of the buttons or hooks are not large enough to pass a tapestry needle through or if the project yarn is bulky. If that is the case, use thread or a finer gauge yarn in a natural, not synthetic, fiber.

Blocking

I believe that the secret to professional looking knits is in the finishing process. In order to avoid "homemade" looking garments, you need to block. There are many methods for blocking, and this is what I have found to be the most successful:

Weave in any loose tails you may have. Thoroughly soak the garment in cold water; you can also add a light laundry wash such as Soak. Gently squeeze out the excess water and lightly roll in a towel if necessary. Place the piece on a blocking mat or board. I use a blocking board with a measurement grid, so I can easily map the dimensions of the piece without using a tape measure. At any rate, you need to have a flat surface that you can pin into. Shape the piece to match the measurements on the schematic and pin in place.

If the instructions say to "lightly block" that usually refers to a piece that has ribbing or cables and means to not stretch the piece, which will cause the elasticity and stitch pattern to flatten. If you do happen to stretch ribbing out too far during the blocking process, you can always spray the ribbed section with water and gently push back into place. At this point, I usually pin down the sides, but if the edges are flat and to the dimensions required, then pinning is not necessary.

Before blocking, lace does not remotely resemble what the finished product should be. So when blocking lace, I stretch the piece pretty aggressively in order to open up all of the yarnover holes and straighten out the decreases, then I pin down the edges using as many pins as possible to create the desired shape— scallops, triangles, etc.

Finally I add steam using a pressure steamer. I hold the steamer a couple of inches away from the fabric and apply steam thoroughly. This really sets the pattern and the stitches in place and helps in retaining the shape of the item even after wearing. Blocking and steaming your gauge swatch eliminates the possibility that the yarn for your project will not respond well to steam.

Abbreviations

2yo	*Double yarnover:* Wrap yarn around LH needle twice; on next row, drop first yarnover to make a single elongated yarnover
3/3 LC	Sl 3 sts to cn and hold in front; k1, p1, k1; k1, p1, k1 from cn
3/3 LC Inc	Sl 3 sts to cn and hold in front; k3, M2; k3 from cn— 2 sts inc'd
3/3 LC-Rib	Sl 3 sts to cn and hold in front; k1, p1, k1; k1; p1, k1 from cn
3/3 RC	Sl 3 sts to cn and hold in back; k1, p1, k1; k1, p1, k1 from cn
3/3 RC-Rib	Sl 3 sts to cn and hold in back; k1, p1, k1; k1, p1, k1 from cn
4/4 RC Inc	Sl 4 sts to cn and hold in back; k4, M2; k4 from cn— 2 sts inc'd
5/5 LC	Sl 5 sts to cn and hold in front; k5; k5 from cn
5/5 LC Inc	Sl 5 sts to cn and hold in front; k5, M2; k5 from cn— 2 sts inc'd
5/5 LC-Purl Rib	Sl 5 sts to cn and hold in front; [p1, k1] twice, p1; [p1, k1] twice, p1 from cn
5/5 LC-Rib	Sl 5 sts to cn and hold in front, [k1, p1] twice, k1; [k1, p1] twice, k1 from cn
5/5 RC	Sl 5 sts to cn and hold in back, k5; k5 from cn.
5/5 RC-Purl Rib	Sl 5 sts to cn and hold in back, [p1, k1] twice, p1; [p1, k1] twice, p1 from cn
5/5 RC-Rib	Sl 5 sts to cn and hold in back, [k1, p1] twice, k1; [k1, p1] twice, k1 from cn
approx	Approximately
beg	Beginning

BO	Bind off
Cable M1	Pass 3rd st on LH needle over 2nd and 1st sts; k1, M1, k1
Cable yo	Pass 3rd st on LH needle over 2nd and 1st sts; k1, yo, k1
CC	Contrasting color
cdd	*Central double decrease:* Sl 2 sts as if to knit 2 tog, knit 1, pass slipped sts over—2 sts dec'd
CL	*Cluster:* Sl number of sts indicated to cn; wrap yarn clockwise 3 times around sts on cn; purl sts from cn
cm	Centimeter
CO	Cast on
cont	Continue
dec	Decrease(ing)
g	Gram
inc	Increase(ing)
k	Knit
kf&b	Knit into front, then back, of same st—1 st inc'd
k2tog	Knit 2 sts together; right-slanting dec—1 st dec'd
k2tog-T	Sl 1 st as if to purl, sl 1 st as if to knit, return 2 sts to LH needle, knit 2 sts together; twisted, right-slanting dec—1 st dec'd
k3tog-T	Sl 2 sts as if to purl, sl 1 st as if to knit, return 3 sts to LH needle, knit 3 sts together; twisted right-slanting dec—2 sts dec'd
LH	Left-hand
m	Meter(s)

Prepare and Have Fun!

Knitting patterns are like recipes—make sure to have all of your "ingredients" gathered and techniques clarified ahead of time to ensure success. Before starting a project, it is important to read through the entirety of the pattern. Confirm that you have a thorough understanding of how the piece is constructed before casting on. It may also be helpful to make a list of abbreviations used that you are not familiar with. Lastly, learn any techniques that are new to you by practicing them on a swatch in order to avoid frustration. A little preparation will make your knitting experience enjoyable and rewarding!

MC	Main color
meas	Measures
M1, M1L	*Make 1, Make 1 Left:* Insert LH needle, from front to back, under strand of yarn that runs between next st on LH and last st on RH needle; knit this st through back loop; left-slanting inc—1 st inc'd
M1P	*Make 1 Purl:* Insert LH needle, from front to back, under strand of yarn that runs between next st on LH needle and last st on RH needle; purl this st through back loop—1 st inc'd
M1R	*Make 1 Right:* Insert LH needle, from back to front, under strand of yarn which runs between next st on LH needle and last st on RH needle; knit this st through front loop; right-slanting inc—1 st inc'd
M2	*Make 2:* Insert LH needle, from front to back, under strand of yarn that runs between next st on LH needle and last st on RH needle; knit this st through back loop, then front loop—2 sts inc'd
p	Purl
patt(s)	Pattern(s)
p2tog	Purl 2 sts together—1 st dec'd
pm	Place marker
psso	Pass slipped stitch over
rem	Remain(ing)
rep	Repeat
RH	Right-hand
RS	Right side(s)
skp	Sl 1 st as if to knit, knit 1 st, pass slipped st over; left-slanting dec—1 st dec'd

skp-T	Sl 1 st as if to purl, knit 1 st, pass slipped st over; twisted left-slanting dec—1 st dec'd
sk2p	Sl 1 st as if to knit, knit 2 sts together, pass slipped st over; left-slanting dec—2 sts dec'd
sk2p-T	Sl 1 st as if to purl, knit 2 st together, pass slipped st over; twisted left-slanting dec—2 sts dec'd
Sl	Slip
sl m	Slip marker
ssk	Sl 2 sts individually as if to knit, then knit those 2 sts together through the back loops; left-slanting dec—1 st dec'd
sssk	Sl 3 sts individually as if to knit, then knit those 3 sts together through the back loops; left-slanting dec—2 sts dec'd
st(s)	Stitch(es)
St st	Stockinettte stitch: Knit on RS rows and purl on WS rows.
tbl	Through back loop
tog	Together
wyib	With yarn in back
wyif	With yarn in front
WS	Wrong side
yd(s)	Yard(s)
w&t	Wrap and turn
WS	Wrong side
yd(s)	Yard(s)
yo	Yarn over

Special Techniques

These are techniques used repeatedly in the patterns. Photos are included for further clarification.

Provisional Cast-on

The provisional cast-on provides a cast-on with a set of live stitches along the edge. This enables a piece to be started in the middle, then worked out in opposite directions so the ends will be congruous. When the first half is complete, the provisional cast-on stitches are "unzipped," placed back on a needle, and worked in the opposite direction. *Note: After unzipping the stitches, you will always have one stitch fewer than what was originally casted on, which requires an increase made when working the first row of the second half.*

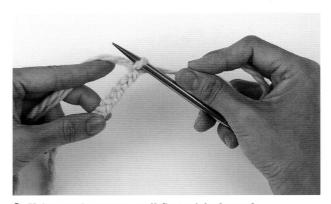

2. Insert knitting needle through "bump" on back of chain.

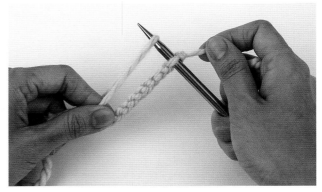

3. Using project yarn, pull first stich through.

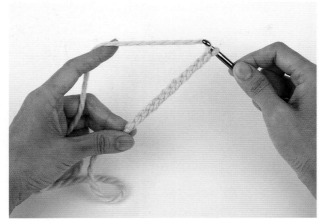

1. With crochet hook and waste yarn, make a chain several stitches longer than the desired cast-on.

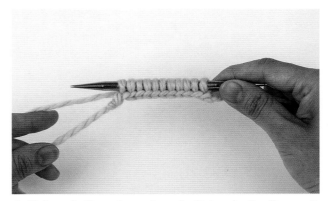

4. Pick up indicated number of stitches in the "bumps" on back of chain. Your provisional cast-on is complete, and you may continue with the pattern.

5. When indicated in pattern, "unzip" the crochet chain and place the live stitches on needle or holder.

3-Needle Join

The 3-needle join is used to join two separate layers of knitted fabric together into one working layer by holding the layers parallel to each other and knitting them together.

1. Hold needles parallel in left hand with right sides of both pieces facing.

2. Insert needle into top stitch on front needle, then top stitch on back needle.

3. Knit together a stitch from the front needle with one from the back. (continued)

4. *Knit together a stitch from the front and back needles. Repeat from * across.

2. Insert needle into top stitch on front needle, then top stitch on back needle.

3-Needle Bind-Off

The 3-needle bind-off joins two separate pieces of knitted fabric together while binding off at the same time, in order to avoid sewing seams during finishing.

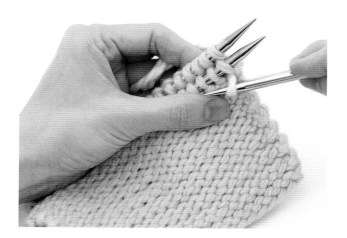

1. Hold needles parallel in left hand with right sides of both pieces together or facing each other, according to pattern directions.

3. Knit together a stitch from the front needle with one from the back.

4. Repeat previous step, so you have 2 stitches on the right-hand needle. Insert left-hand needle into second stitch on the right-hand needle.

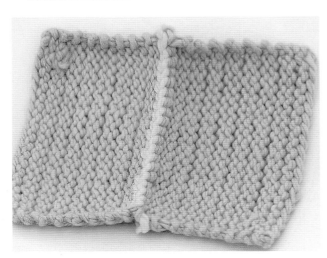

5. Lift that stitch up and over the first stitch and off the needle to bind off.

6. *Knit together a stitch from the front and back needles, and slip the first stitch over the second to bind off. Repeat from * across, then fasten off last stitch.

Short-Row Shaping

This technique is used to form triangles of knitting as worked in the beveled end of a scarf. Shaping with short rows eliminates the uneven edge that occurs when you bind off in a series of stitches. It is a two-step process where you work a partial row of stitches, followed by a "wrap and turn," then work back in the opposite direction. The second step is hiding the wrapped stitches, which may occur all in one row or with every short row set, depending on the direction of the angle; this closes the gap formed when the work is turned.

Wrap and Turn (w&t)

Work to the last stitch of the short row; if the last stitch is a knit stitch, then follow the directions for working on the Knit Side or if the last stitch is a purl stitch, then follow the directions for the Purl Side.

Knit Side

1. With the yarn in back, slip the next stitch purlwise from the left needle to the right needle.

2. Bring the yarn to the front between the two needles. (continued)

3. Slip the first stitch on the right needle back to the left needle and bring the yarn to the back between the two needles.

2. Bring the yarn to the back between the two needles.

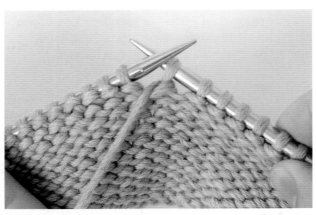

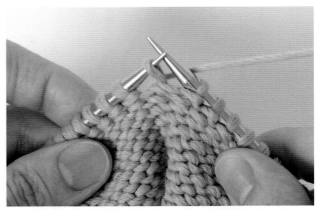

4. Turn the work and complete the row in the reverse direction.

3. Slip the first stitch on the right needle back to the left needle and bring the yarn to the back between the two needles.

Purl Side

4. Turn the work and complete the row in the reverse direction.

1. With the yarn in front, slip the next stitch purlwise from the left needle to the right needle.

Hiding the Wraps

When you have completed your short row sets, as you work across on the next row, you will hide the wraps as you come to them, as instructed below.

Knit Stitch

1. Pick up the wrap from front to back with the right needle.

2. Insert the right needle into the wrapped stitch (first stitch on the left needle) and knit the wrap and the wrapped stitch together.

Purl Stitch

1. Pick up the wrap from back to front with the right needle.

2. Place the wrap on the left needle and purl the wrap and the wrapped stitch together.

Acknowledgments

I would like to thank my family, Scott, Teddy, and Claire (also one of my lovely models), for all of your patience and support while I was noticeably absent so many times in my presence and attention during the production of this book. Charlotte, you were always there with your sage advice, both technical and personal, your keen eye in keeping me in line, and, most of all, for being my loudest and most enthusiastic cheerleader. Thank you, Aliene, for all of the late-night calls and taking care of my family like nobody else could so I could get some work done. A heartfelt thank you to Misty, for realizing my vision in photographs and adding to it your special touch. Kevin and Claire, thank you for capturing all of the detail in the tutorial photos. Pam H., I appreciate your patience and advice in editing this book. To all of my beautiful models and to Theresa, Alison, and Katie, who helped make them even more beautiful, I can't thank you enough.

I always use Nicky Epstein's *Knitted Flowers* as my resource for all things floral embellishment. For stitch patterns, I turn to Barbara Walker's *A Treasury of Knitting Patterns*. For extraordinary colorwork patterns, I use Margaret Radcliffe's *The Essential Guide to Color Knitting Techniques*.

I want to thank the following generous companies for providing yarn support:
Blue Sky Alpacas
Spud and Chloë
Shibui Knits
Madelinetosh
O-Wool
Malabrigo
Swans Island
Cascade
Anzula
Purl Soho
Rowan

For unique buttons and closures, I shop at Textile Garden.com.

Photographs: Misty Matz
Technical editor: Charlotte Quiggle
Hair and makeup: Theresa Huang Makeup & Hair Design
Hair: Alison Chang
Makeup: Katie Wong

Models: Makayla Dembowski
Graycen Jones
Claire Powers
Kennedy Wischmeyer
Miranda Wolford
Sadie Wood